How To Analyze People:

Learn Beginners' Techniques For Speed Reading People, Analyze Personality Types And Human Behavior Psychology Instantly, How To Interpret Verbal Communication And Patterns

Joe Silva

Table of Contents

Introduction

Buying this book means you are going to know everything about analyzing people in every aspect. Whether you are meeting an individual for the first time or the last time, their behavior will not change which is being developed since time. Indeed, reading people is a superb way to make yourself come in a comfortable zone which another person can't even think of.

Varied personalities have different nature which only depends upon the past or present situation in personal or professional life. Some individuals have a nature of keeping things locked inside; whereas, other classes of individuals have a habit of saying everything and anything on the spot. This is what you can judge by their body gestures and tone of the voice.

From the first moment, you meet any individual they consciously or subconsciously analyze you. Now the question arises what is the main motive of this judgment?

Maybe they want to figure out what type of personality you are or you can say they have done mastery on it and want to gain practical knowledge- whatever be the reason. Notwithstanding, analyzing people is an art by which you come to know the opponent person before interacting.

The secret inside this book will offer you a clear picture of the different nature of human beings. Moreover, you will come to know how different individuals react to the same situation differently.

Despite having incredible schooling and getting a higher education, no one taught us how to judge people before getting fully engaged with them. We have been taught how to pass an examination with an excellent grade, but what about getting full on full marks on judging people. This is what this book will tell you.

The main purpose of this book is to take a deep dive through a journey of different people's nature and this would help any personality to understand the opponent person very well. Other than this, after reading this book" How to analyze people," the reader can develop skills to observe and understand others before they become a hurdle in your life.

There are numerous scientifically rectified techniques that help someone to become a better person who is liked by everyone. In this book, I have penned down various things regards to human personality that might help you to recognize the inner clever clog in you for becoming more and more innovative in understanding life in a better way. So, pack up your bags for a dramatic change in your life. Which is obvious for the betterment of yourself!

Chapter 1: How to Read People?

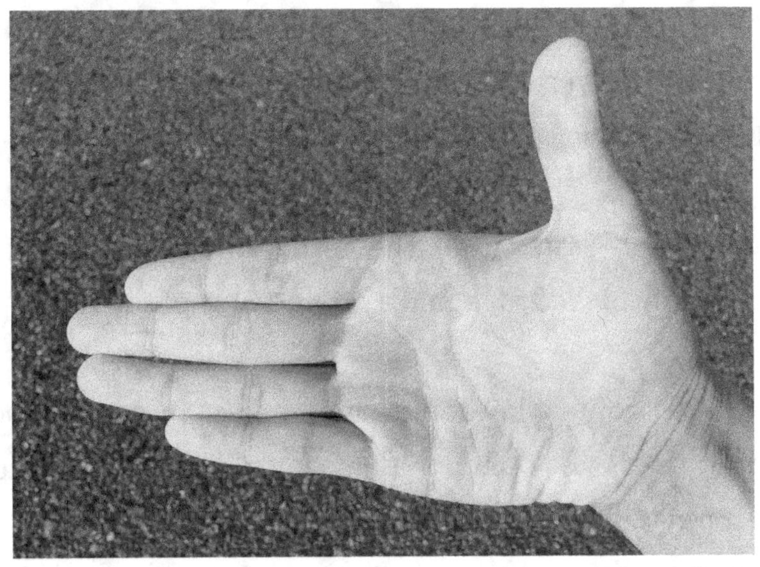

How things would go if you have the power of reading people's mind? The answer is perfect- no one will give a chance to anyone to say something. It can happen with the help of intuition, or if you are not so perspective, then the last option left with you is learning to read people.

But don't get freaked out!

This book is not about reading minds, it is all about what other people want to say or think about another's personality. It is just sensing which makes all the difference. The capability to read people by their body language and voice tone is going to affect your personal, professional, and social life.

Innumerable people like to learn how to read people by which they can be on the safe side or with the help of that person, their near and dear one come in a comfort zone. According to research, the power of body language is more powerful than any other verbal or non-verbal language.

MIT media lab stated that the result of negotiation can be predicted only by body language around 87% of the time.

Most of the people who don't have interest in reading people think that the result of body language or voice tone eventually depends upon the guesses or myth, not on real research.

Being perspective regards to another person's feelings and thoughts is a very crucial skill which is going to strengthen the interpersonal relationship for long life; though all individuals have different personalities with varied thinking, attitude to tackle situations, and many more.

Talking about another side of reading people- it's not about understanding what they say, rather it is about who they are. Because people don't say what they actually are, but they say what the opposite person wants to listen.

In the art of reading people, surrender any past preconceptions, emotional baggage because it will stop you from seeing another person clearly as to what actually he/she is. While reading your boss, your colleague, or any near and dear one, you have to surrender biases. In the path of reading others, follow the old style of watching invisible. This way you can utilize your time and energy to look further which can happen in the future.

It is a fact that people can judge 55% of the information through non-verbal communication. As one of the Australians who is one of the best body language experts said that mimics and gestures can unmask the person and can actually tell you what they really think or feel.

Read people like an FBI agent!

With the advent of the technological era, we can say that our interaction with people in order to know about them is peaking. In our day to day life, you send hundreds of text messages and emails but the main motive remains in between. That is knowing people what they actually are. Our face to face context is limiting because of a sedentary lifestyle and busy professional life.

According to MIT experts, words account for only 7% of the real communication, so when an individual starts paying attention towards other aspects of the body like body language and tone, then he/she can take an advantageous ground over others.

Techniques of reading people

The bright side of this book is it will tell you some techniques of reading people. They are as follows: -

These are the body gestures which can help you to read another person's intentions. In the process of reading people, there are two sides to it; that is- encoding and decoding.

Encoding is sending cues to the other person in the form of different actions and reactions.

Decoding is the capability to read an individual's emotions and feelings in order to predict what he/she might be thinking.

Technique-1
He/she closes eyes while talking

Hey guys, have you seen any person who closes his/her eyes while talking to someone?
Well, I have seen as he wants to hide something from the outside world. It means he/she might be tired of your company. By closing his/her eyes, they want to show just go away and let me live and enjoy my life.

Biting arms of their sunglasses

I have seen many individuals who always bite the arms of their sunglasses. But I always think about why they do it. Now it will get the answer that they are worried about something about their personal or professional life. If you come across that kind of people, then try to encourage or motivate them that every problem has a solution if you will think positively.

Rubbing his own chin

This is all about people thinking to take some decision, but not able to decide that is it right or wrong. However, they often look here and there and don't notice that someone is looking at them because of deep thought.

Examine the position of the arms

Have you seen this body language in people? When I use to see this gesture, I always thought that maybe they are very comfortable in their position. But, after research, it is found that crossed arms is the sign of not feeling good regards to something.

So, the next time you see this gesture ask that person for what you are not feeling good and he/she will be surprised to know how you know this.

Leaning back on the chair

This posture is very common when some meeting is going on. Means they are tired of the conversation and want to go outside or stop it. Perhaps, they are not comfortable.

Rubbing hands

In the winter season, people usually rub their hands in order to generate heat which in turn helps the body to feel hot. But normally, this sign signifies something positive is happening in their lives.

Hope is that thing which every person wants to live with which can help to predict the future.

How they present face

This gesture of the body is more open to the people if they understand. It usually signifies attraction. When men or women want to attract each other, they present themselves in such a way that the opposite person gets attracted like straightening his/her back, etc.

Watch for hand signals

The hands of a person seek essential nonverbal cue in the process of reading people. Different positions of the hand show something varied like: -

Hand in the pocket or on the head indicates nervousness to outright deception

Supporting the head with the hands by clicking elbow on the table means he/she is trying to focus

Handshake with a palm facing the floor

When a person holds your hand or you will hold someone's hand from below, then it shows that you are ready to help that person in any situation.

Observe people's feet

Apart from the body, the feet also show some non-verbal cues to indicate something to another person. The main motive of indicating their feelings through feet is that they are able to control their body and facial expressions.

Moreover, if the person is interacting in a group and if his/her foot is towards you, then he/she is thinking positive regards to you.

Eye to eye contact

The eye works as the window to read the feelings and emotions of a person. According to the situation, eyes show a different feeling which tells us everything about that person.

Keeping feet on the table

I think this gesture of the body everyone can understand. It expresses numerous things regards to that person like disrespect, bad manners, trying to show there is no value of the boss and many more.

Studies state that if a person feels comfortable sitting like this, then he/she can but only at home.

The study of reading people in the form of body gestures is very vast which is not going to stop. The expressions which are listed above are some of them and basic by which you or I can understand the opposite person's feelings.

Technique-2
Listen to your intuition

An individual can tune someone other than body language or facial expressions which is what your guts feel. A person's intuition can tell a richer story than any other thing.

Always listen to what your guts say

Listening to the guts is very crucial especially when you are meeting a person for the first time. It will offer you a non-rational reaction which you never think of. Your own guts tell you that story which actually you are feeling while interacting with that person.

So, listen to your guts and make a decision whether you can trust a person or not.

Sensing the person's presence

Everyone can understand easily. It means when someone enters inside, what is the actual atmosphere that came up and surrounded you.

Try to analyze whether the atmosphere is friendly which attracts everyone or it will be distracting.

Always pay attention to flashes of insight

One time or the other, you can feel ah-ha feeling about the individual. It's a warning because it will come in a flash. However, you will miss it as a person's mind to start thinking about the different things so rapidly.

Try not to make assumptions

It is a fact that assumptions result in misunderstanding. Coming to the result before knowing that person always brings you in trouble.

The key is to read people like a pro in which you have to relax and think positive in order to analyze people.

Practice watching people

It is a well-known proverb that practice makes a man perfect so this also applies to read people too. If you want to win over others, start practicing watching people like watching shows on TV with mute volume. Try to judge people by their facial expressions and body language without hearing their voice. After that, watch that show again and judge yourself if your judgment is right or wrong.

Notice people's words or the language they use while talking

While talking to someone like your friend, colleague, boss or any other person, just listen to them carefully. To illustrate this- let me give you an example. When someone does his/her praise themselves, these type of people relies on other people to boost their self-image.

Be objective and open-minded

The first and foremost step in starting reading people is having an open mind. Don't let your emotions or past experiences come in between while analyzing people. However, if you are reading people easily, then there are chances of misreading people too.

In this world of colorful people, it is a very essential thing to read people from deep which can help you in understanding them better. The good news is that the ability to read people is good, but keep one thing in mind while reading people what to look for is essential.

Outcomes of reading body language

Reading body language engages numerous legitimate and natural results which are very beneficial for the people.

Social benefits-In our social life, studying body language offers us many benefits by which you can save yourself. Interpreting body language offers us the opportunity to understand who may be a threat, who is in need of help, and which person is acting in a productive manner or not.

Professional benefits- Judging your boss or your colleague is a very good idea which will tell you what they are expecting from you. But in the routine of expectations, they can expect something negative according to you. So, in this case, you have to be conscious and tackle that situation in a positive way. Other than this, the art of judging people in one way or the other helps in strengthening the relationship in professional life.

Overall there are innumerable benefits of reading people, so study the art of reading people and get ready to stay positive and make everyone positive around.

Chapter 2: What is Human Behavior?

When I or you try to understand humans on how they act or interact to a particular situation, this is known to be human behavior. Numerous experts and researchers are trying to make up why humans react to a particular situation in the opposite way.

Psychology is the study of human behavior which tells us that human behavior consists of two things- one is the nature of person how he/she behaves and the second one is the nature of any situation by which he/she has to react.

Human behavior is classified into various types by which you can understand which type of person they are: -

Molecular and Molar behavior

When sudden reaction comes on behalf of a person, it is a molecular behavior; For example- when you fail in an exam; that behavior which comes all of a sudden like alas. In this, you haven't prepared yourself to face a situation like this.

Moler behavior is right opposite to molecular behavior in which you are fully prepared to react if something happens. Like what to do when earthquakes occur or counter-attack.

Overt and covert behavior

Overt behavior is that in which the human being shows to the outside world. For example, listening to the talk with full focus but not implementing actually.

Covert behavior is not visible from outside which occurs inside the human body. For example, in order to change him/her, people change from inside in order to be the best.

Voluntary and involuntary behavior

That type of behavior which depends upon human wants like talking, walking, writing, etc is voluntary behavior. On this behavior, humans have full control.

Human behavior that is happening naturally in the human body like the internal movement of the heart, taking oxygen, etc is involuntary.

Moreover, every behavior is interrelated to each other in one way or the other. It also depends upon our genetic-makeup, culture, individual values, and attitudes.

Now let's talk about human behavior regards to the present-day situation. As technology is reaching its heights, the behavior of humans is changing tremendously. They are getting self-centered in their lifestyle neglecting various aspects or you can say relations.

It is a fact that human behavior is different in personal and professional life; but nowadays, professional life is disturbing the personal life.

Due to these issues, stress has become a very common problem.

So, what exactly is human behavior?

Well, it is a combination of act-think-feel.

However, our actions what we show to the world will become our routine behavior. No matter if it is right or wrong according to the situation or people, but we have to take action without thinking about what others feel. In this way of reacting, the person who reads people's mind and body language specialists can easily understand what he/she is thinking about.

Cognitions are our behavior

Our own cognitions describe thoughts and mental images you carry with you and it can be verbal and nonverbal. Moreover, if one person has to remember they have to do a certain work, then it is verbal cognition.

Apart from that, if a person is thinking and imagining that his/her house will look beautiful after renovation, it is non-verbal cognition.

Emotions are our behavior

Eventually, a small conscious behavior is characterized by mental activity and it is not featured by reasoning and knowledge.

So, everything is connected to behaviors like emotions, cognitions, and actions. The proper use of all three makes the world around you in a better way.

Features of human behavior

Adaptable to social rules and regulations in order to run their personal life

Language and understanding results in better feelings and emotions

With the help of human behavior, different persons have the capability to learn more knowledge

With proper drive or aim, human behavior can help them to attain their desired aim

Education and knowledge are one of the most essential parts of human behavior which can be easily achieved

Ways to understand human behavior

In analyzing people, human behavior plays a very essential role which can help understand humans in a precise manner. Human nature is influenced by all kinds of products like genes, culture, surrounding atmosphere, and not the least, upbringing. As time passes, human beings actively process and interact in an ever-changing environment.

In order to survive in this globe, humans have to learn a certain kind of behavior. Here you will come to that human behavior which makes survival in this competitive world.

Introspection methods

It is also known as self-observation method and in this introspection means to look within. A person can easily understand their own inner feelings and emotions in a better way than any other person. So, in this, the person him/herself works as the reporter.

For example- a child can report his pain in a better way than his/her mother. In this, the child's feelings come from inside and then only he/she is able to tell which helps the doctor in offering the best treatment to the child.

So, this method of introspection works best according to the child.

Observation method

This method of observation is like reading people what they are doing or by their physical actions. In this, the other person will observe and collect the information. For example: in a class, the teacher observes the behavior of the child when they are with friends and with teachers.

This method is mainly used by doctors in the treatment of patients who are mentally ill in a natural setting. Because the patients are not aware regards to that they are getting observed.

It also goes for people who are good at reading or who want to learn the art of reading people. They usually see their actions and reactions from far and come to the conclusion what type of person he/she is.

Experimental method

It is the most objective way to understand human behavior in which proper experiments are conducted in the laboratories. Mainly, in the experiments, the effect of the independent variable on the dependent variable is studied in order to get the result.

This experiment is conducted through the following steps: -

The doctors identify the problem

Hypothesis is formulated

Process of designing the experiment takes place

Test of the hypothesis will go

Analysis of result

Lastly, doctors interpret the result to come to a conclusion

In this, the result of the experiment is verified by the repetition of the same method again and again.

Case history method

This method is very common in hospitals and educational settings. When a person is admitted in the hospital, the nurse frequently collects all the data which is called the past history. And most essentially with the help of friends or relatives, they come to verify any changes during this period.

This method is very useful in studying human behavior with the passage of time so that they can come to the conclusion.

Survey method

Mainly survey method is used in companies so that they come to know about their products outside. But nowadays it is also used in studying human behavior. People in and around give the feedback of the person whose behavior is to be studied.

Moreover, this method is also used in medical professions like awakening people about diseases, health facilities available, etc.

Genetic method

It is also known as a development method. Our today's behavior sometimes results in our past experiences means the person's development aspects. Maybe that person has gone through such a situation which makes the individual behave like this.

To get the best result out of it since childhood till now, the variations in their life are studied.

Testing method

By the psychologist, different tests are conducted related to their hobbies, abilities, attitudes, adjustments so that they come to know the real culprit of this kind of behavior.

So understanding human behavior is not a tough task. We just have to understand everything in regards to that person. This book on "HOW TO ANALYZE PEOPLE" covers all the topics related to human behavior, reading people, and many others.

How to understand yourself?

Before understanding other ways of behaving and altogether studying human behavior, it is very essential to understand yourself better, because it is the key to understand another person in a better way.

As you keep up going through responsibilities, many obligations come in between and there is a time when we stare in the mirror saying "who I am"? In order to achieve your future plans, you yourself get invisible.

Indeed, if you don't understand yourself, then the time is not far when you become easily attracted and pushed into that lifestyle which doesn't represent you. Means you are leading that life what others want you to live.

If you want to understand yourself, just ask these few questions to yourself which will make you understand you in a better way and which will unlock your potential. They are: -

What are your strengths?

Do you offer better results in working alone or in a team?

What type of personality you are?

What are the things that set you apart from others?

Are you comfortable in taking risks?

What's more crucial for you- a family or a career?

Are you patient or impatient?

Do you say yes or no too much?

These are among the numerous questions which you can ask yourself to steer your life in the right direction.

Now in the below discussion, you will come to know how you can understand yourself in a better way in order to read people; because if you yourself understand in an excellent way, then only you are able to analyze the other person.

Meditation

Take out some time from your sedentary lifestyle and meditate in the morning or before sleeping. However, just focus on the thoughts which are coming and going into your mind. Keep in mind to practice this in a peaceful environment and notice various ideas which come naturally to you.

This way when you connect with inner peace, it helps you to understand yourself the best.

This is a very common approach which works best in understanding yourself.

If you want to achieve your goal, take risks

Life goes nowhere if you have a constant fear of failure and you don't take any step in order to get success. As an individual, accept that you are not going to be perfect all the time you try.

Furthermore, if you take risks as an adventure then you will be embracing yourself in every type of journey you'll take. So, by exploring alternative routes, try to take risks which will make you understand yourself perfectly; and by your personal experience, you will be able to analyze people.

Focus on what inspires you

Have you ever noticed that what are the things or people that inspire you the most? If yes, then you are on the right path of understanding yourself. On the other hand, you can give advice to other people also regarding this.

Evaluate your strengths and weaknesses

You can come up to be a better you if you consider your strengths and weaknesses. Try to use your strength in a better way and make your weaknesses also your strength. Moreover, take what others say about your weaknesses. Then you will become a better person and understand yourself.

Keep on learning

Surge your knowledge while watching motivational videos, podcasts, and taking general information which you wouldn't try otherwise. In the process of understanding yourself, make your mind active and keep yourself engaged in different activities so that you come to know about your likes and dislikes, what you feel challenging, what you want to explore further, and many more other things.

Make yourself free to do creative activities

You would be very surprised to know when you free yourself and try your best to do creative tasks. In this, your imagination makes you feel what are your inner strengths.

Well, from inside you might think that I want to do this or that, so this activity will finally give you an outlet. Creative activities can be many like coloring, painting, playing music, and numerous others.

Do a character writing exercise

When writers start writing a book beforehand, they do some writing exercises so that they eventually go into the character or you can say understand them in a better way. Ask some questions to yourself and by answering these questions, you will slowly start understanding yourself. The questions can be: -

How are you different from other people around you?

What is the most beautiful thing which had happened in your life since now?

What is the purpose of your life, and numerous others?

Think about your life's journey until now

As a person, look at your past and see your present attitude and behavior. What had happened to you over your lifetime which has affected you to act like this. However, if you see this, you can reveal a lot about yourself and be able to understand yourself much more than before.

Examine yourself when you interact with other people

Try to see yourself when you talk to other people- do you tend to put them down? Every individual has his choice of people whom they want to interact. So, see this in you and overall this behavior will teach you everything about yourself.

Practice positivity

Sometimes due to numerous situations, loving yourself is hard to do, but it is the most essential aspect in understanding yourself. Accept yourself what you are- like your weaknesses, likes, dislikes, and many more.

After that, start speaking or writing positive thoughts and quotes about yourself to be extra bold.

Be true to yourself

In the process of knowing yourself, always be true to yourself if you want to understand yourself and want to yield good results. Because if you don't accept things the way they are about yourself, then it is very hard to continue your path of knowing yourself.

Values

Values such as thinking about others, helping others, being innovative, financial security, and much more are the ultimate guide to decision making and motivating yourself to attain the goals.

A study states that just writing and thinking about your values can result in healthy actions which can benefit both you and your near and dear ones.

Observe yourself how you react in varied situations

When things get really tough on your part how you will react in that situation or when it is in favor of you in these cases your restrained parts of the character come out. After that, think that have you reacted accurately to such situations which will automatically help you to understand yourself in a better way.

When it comes to understanding yourself, no one will do it for you as you know your worst and best things. The process of knowing yourself will take some time but after this process is over, you will come out to be a perfect example for others. Utilize all the steps which are discussed above and follow the path of changing yourself.

Chapter 3: What is Human Personality?

Almost every now and then, we try to assess and describe people according to their personality which they display in front of others. At that time, our wordings are like what is a great personality?

And we also say that his/her personality is like his dad. So, in our daily routine, we might talk about human personality which creates a long-lasting impact on the other person.

Furthermore, an individual's personality is inclusive of traits and patterns which clearly influence their behavior, thoughts, motivation, and emotions. Personality is that thing which drives a human being to behave as he/she does. However, human personality also depends upon on the genetic factors which you show to the outside world.

What makes someone who they are? Each individual has their own idea of what type of personality they figure. That's why psychologists have categorized human personality into various types.

Other than the professional atmosphere, there are environmental factors that can play an essential role in the development and expression of human personality. Means from childhood till adolescence how kids are brought up usually depend upon on their parents and their styles. Indeed, different norms and expectations of the culture make a human personality unique and attractive.

So, let's put some light on the major components of human personality which make a human being a perfect person: -

Consistency- In many individuals, there is a recognizable order and regularity to behaviors. Means people act in the same way and in a similar way in all the situations.

Psychological and physiological- Human personality is made up of a psychological construct, but experts consider it as a combination of biological processes.

Impacts human behavior and actions- Human personality is not just how we respond and act in certain situations. Rather, it has come up with more unique benefits according to your past experiences. Means it constrains us to act in a certain way which maybe you don't like.

Shows multiple sides- A personality is not just our behavior with others or with ourselves, but it is a combination of our own thoughts, feelings, emotions, social interactions.

Now let's talk about personality traits regards to an individual which make them unique and different: -

Openness
Conscientiousness
Extraversion
Agreeableness
Neuroticism

These five traits act as an ingredient to make the human personality.

Openness- Open people are highly adventurous and open in front of others. Indeed, they are very curious to know new things and always appreciate art, imagination, and good thinking. The main aim of open people is to add spice in their or other's life.

Apart from that, an individual who is not open has the opposite habits. They want to confine themselves to their usual behavior and habits.

Conscientiousness- The conscientious people are more responsible and are well organized. These kinds of people are independent, focused to achieve their goal, and well-disciplined. Moreover, they will not backfire any type of journey which comes in their life ever.

The people who are low in conscientiousness are more spontaneous and free-wheeling. They are very careless towards their life. This trait helps in achieving goals in school or college life and in the job also.

Extraversion- The people who have extraversion trait in them are very sociable, chatty, and draw energy from the crowd. They are very assertive and cheerful in social interactions.

Furthermore, the opposite of extraversion is an introvert who wants to spend time alone with less social interaction. Their nature is very shy and but they are perfectly charming in the parties.

Agreeableness- This trait measures a person's heart in the form of kindness. They are likely to be trusted by anyone and are very helpful and compassionate.

Opposite to that, people are cold and suspicious, as do not cooperate easily.

Neuroticism- These kinds of people take more tension and easily slip into anxiety and depression. One way or the other, they find things to worry about. Due to these factors, a neuroticism individual is linked to bad health habits.

Types of personalities

Have you ever considered why human beings do what they do?

Why people react to the same situation in a different way?

In your life till now, have you tried to understand anyone maybe your loved ones?

And how in spite of different natures you get along with people at home or at work? The answer to all these questions will be discussed in the below discussion which makes you understand why it happens and how you cooperate in these types of situations.

Every individual is unique in his own from head to toe, and despite all that, it is very surprising to recognize any person's personality. Psychologists have boxed human personality into varied categories so that it is easy to identify. Moreover, all these personality types tell us how individuals perceive the world internally and how they interact with others in different situations.

As we all are different, and this difference makes our place and life more interesting. That's why some individuals get easily successful in their life but, some take time. Have you imagined that what happens if all the persons were the same?

To understand this, let me give you an example, just imagine a house is on fire and out of many people some are rushing towards the house to evacuate it, some of them are making arrangements of the ambulance. Other than this, most of the people call the fire brigade. In this scenario, if all the individuals will do only one work, then who will do the other arrangements. This is one of the examples of varied personalities which is very crucial to handle any situation.

Every human being reacts differently in the same situations which are must live life. We are motivated by different personalities, their thoughts, actions, and reactions. That's why numerous humans choose their role models which they want to be like them.

Now the next question arises why it is essential to understand human personality?
Well from an academic point of view, it is very interesting but, if we talk about life then it is much more essential than

academics. The better you understand yourself and the human beings, the more capable you become in dealing with different situations and become more successful.

Understanding human personality is a practical subject so that you yourself maintain your life, deal with varied situations, manage the issues, and most crucially manage and understand your own impact on another person's life.

So, being blind to your own personality leads to these things: -
Negativity inside us remains to unlock; which as a result, becomes a hurdle in getting success
We only focus on our weaknesses, not on the strengths
You can miss the opportunity to play with your strength and improve your negative traits

And you also need to understand the opposite person, which then leads to: -
Understanding another person, you try to interact with that according to the situation
While understanding the whole personality of the individual, you cannot get trapped in their first impression

So, it would be very beneficial to understand human personality which would lead to happiness, growth, and self-development.

Now let's discuss types of human personalities: -

The Duty Fulfillers

This type of personality of people is very reserved and quiet who want to live a peaceful and secure life. Indeed, they feel a sense of duty internally which make them do their work with full motivation so that the task should be the best.

Talking about personal qualities, they are very loyal, faithful, and dependable. They always give importance to honesty and integrity and give preference to their family than their professional life.

In their life, they give importance to traditions and values which they expect from others too. Moreover, for good reason, they are ready to break the law if they want.

On the other hand, they always give importance to promised work which they try to fulfill on time.

In order to fulfill any desired goal, they put a lot of energy in that work so that it would be achieved. They are likely to be uncomfortable expressing affection and emotion to others. However, their strong sense of duty and capability to understand what is to be done in any situation allows them to overcome natural reservations.

Altogether, they are very supportive and caring human beings and they adore their loved ones the most. If they realize that their loved ones need any sort of help, then they come forward to help them whatever the situation may be.

The Guardians

They usually live in a world of facts and concrete needs. Their vision is always clear with regards to the goal which they have to achieve. That's why this type of personality of people steps into a leadership role. Self-confidence and aggressiveness are in them so that they do their best effort in overcoming any hurdle of life.

These individuals take every step with proper care so that there is no chance of mistakes.

Towards the nation, they are a good citizen who always abides by the rules and regulations. People think about them as the pillars of the community. They enjoy the company of family, friends, and other people too which makes them unique and attractive among the other personalities.

Notwithstanding, if they are bogged by stress, they feel very isolated as they are misunderstood and undervalued by others. However, for them, it is very easy to get verbal but sometimes under stress communicating their feelings and emotions gets very difficult. They can do anything to maintain their personal, professional, and social life which another person thinks to be a difficult task. Their approach is always practical, realistic, and dependable.

The Helpers or Caregivers

The helpers are very caring and interpersonal types. They love people and are warmly interested in them. They have inbuilt sensing and judging features by which they usually gather information regards to any person. These types of people have lots of friends and they enjoy their company because of their fun-loving nature and an enthusiastic attitude.

Helpers are very responsible people who take their responsibility very seriously in order to fulfill it. They believe in giving people satisfaction making own way to be happy. Their nature is very sensitive and perceptive regards to others, and can always be counted to lend a helping hand. For them, saying no is quite hard. They live to please others; that's why they often fear rejection from another person's part.

This feeling of rejection counters bitterness and resentment in the long run. Their main focus is on reading people. Indeed, they want to be liked by others and be in control of other individuals.

Other than this, their value system is external by which they form own style of ideas and path which he/she has to follow in the long-run. Their main qualities are warm, sympathetic, tactful, helpful, practical, realistic, well-organized, and energetic.

Caregivers enjoy traditions and security which make them seek a stable life which is rich in contacts like family and friends.

The Performers or Achievers

As the name suggests, they are ready to set the desired goal which they want to achieve and hit the target at once. Their main focus is only on achieving the goal which they accomplish by hook or by crook. Indeed, they live in a world of possibilities where new people and new experiences come in their way.

The performers have excellent interpersonal skills which make them unique and extraordinary. Whatever work they do, they do it with full excitement and finish it.

For them, this entire world is like a stage on which they want to be the center of attention. Entertainment is in their blood which makes the other individuals happy.

Often, they become role models for others who inspire numerous other personalities. Their work approach is practical and they hate routine and structure. They want to work with their own flow while trusting in their own abilities.

When sometimes they get bonded with the stress, they get easily overwhelmed with the negative thoughts and feelings.

They have a tremendous love life and very well-known on how to live a happy life. Side by side they like to bring others along on their fun-loving rides and want to have fun with them.

The Artists

They live in a world of imagination, that's why they are quiet and it is very difficult to know what kind of people they are. They are very kind, gentle, and sensitive while dealing with others. They have a strong affinity towards aesthetics and beauty; that's why they are animal lovers and appreciate nature.

They want to live an independent life and find space for their personal needs.

Moreover, they are action-oriented individuals who believe in doing things practically. They love doing things which are practical in nature and usually get bored with traditional teaching methods.

These kinds of people don't let their life to be controlled by others and they don't like other's life controlled by them.

Indeed, the artist's personality people are likely to not give enough credit to their work which they do very well. Their value system is so strong that they live the life of a perfectionist. And in case any difficulty comes in their life, they tend to judge themselves and come out of it easily.

On the other hand, they give selflessness gift to the world by serving with artistic sensation and their creativity. Life of artistic people is not easy but they work hard to make their life perfect with a richly rewarding experience.

The Thinkers

As the name states, these people live in the globe of theoretical possibilities. They are likely to see things how they may be improved or turning failures into success stories. They are living in confined to their own minds so that they come out with possible solutions to every issue.

Thinkers don't like to lead or control other people. Rather, they are tolerant and flexible in every situation. Indeed, they are very comfortable with those individuals who are old but feel shy meeting new people.

They are usually very independent, unconventional, and original in their attitude. Their thinking pattern is ingenious and unconventional, and that's why they analyze ideas in a unique way. Their way to express themselves is very extraordinary which shows absolute truth. In some cases, these types of people express their well-thought ideas which another individual is not able to understand.

Scientifically their way of thinking is smart and unique which can breakthrough many scientific theories. They are pioneers of new thoughts in society.

The Challengers or the Warriors

They are strong and dominating people who want to rule on the minds of other people. You can say they are natural leaders, assertive, and confident. They have full strength to tackle any situation which comes close to their path.

Moreover, these individuals are masters of their own destiny and always prefer to control people and circumstances.

Other than this, they are honest in every work they do; but side by side, they are featured with bluntness. Often, they are misunderstood by people because of explosive and intense nature which is not liked by the opposite humans. Most of the people fear them as they have a straightforward attitude.

The Protectors

You would find this personality in very few human beings, as it is found rarely. They are gentle, caring and intuitive individuals who live in the world of hidden meaning and possibilities. Out of 100%, only 1% of people have this type of personality. They are pessimistic people who surely find any problem in every situation. These types of humans don't take the risk to trust others in any way and only believe in them.

Sometimes, they show stubbornness and have a tendency to ignore another individual whether they are right or wrong.

This personality could not find peace in them as they always search for something new in order to improve it.

Furthermore, their way of living life is according to them only in which they don't like any interference. The protectors are somehow gentle and easy-going but the thing is they expect much from themselves and the same expectation they tend from another person.

Notwithstanding, their main quality is they show themselves in that area where they can be more creative, innovative and can work independently. They have a great affinity towards art and craft or in the science field in which they show intuition.

The protectors are gifted in such a way in which others are not. They are capable of doing great things which make their life uneasy.

The Scientists

As the name suggests, they believe in doing things carefully with strategic planning. They value intelligence, knowledge, competence, and try to accomplish high standards in this regard. Moreover, their expectations to themselves and from others are same which sometimes is not liked by the people. They are featured as excellent observers who want to gather more and more information and surge their existing knowledge.

Their mind is of an extremely sharp and intelligent person who wants to invent something unique.

The scientists don't show off things and want to remain in the background until and unless there is a great need to come forward.
Talking about their leadership role, they work effectively in that too because of their analytical mind which actually configures the reality of the situation.

These types of people are very ambitious, self-confident, and deliberate, and think long-lasting.

They have a tremendous amount of energy to accomplish new and innovative things which they can use for the benefit of people also. The competent nature gives them the power to attain their desired goal in education or professional sector. In the personal arena, if they practice tolerance, they can lead a more rewarding life.

The Executives
Such people have god-gifted leadership skills and become excellent leaders in any field. They want to live in a world of possibilities where they can challenge every type of situation

which comes in their way. They take charge of people and make them understand the importance of their work in a polite manner.

Indeed, their approach is very focused which make them fit into the corporate world easily and quickly. Their main tendency is to figure out solutions from every problem which comes in their way.

They generally see every small to big thing from a long-range perspective and try to find plans to turn the problem into a solution.

The executives love to interact with different people at every point of time to gain new experiences. As they have a very forceful and dynamic presence, because of self-confidence and verbal communication skills. Numerous gifts have given by God to them in the form of internal power that's why they remain balanced in their life. They are assertive, innovators, long-range thinkers to translate excellent possibilities into outcome.

The Doer

This personality likes quick action and immediate results. They lead enthusiastic and exciting lives in the world of action. Indeed, they take a number of risks in their life and get their hands dirty. In order to solve any issue, they pick up small cues which no one notices in the form of facial expression and stance.

The doers are straight forward and fast taking people who love drama and style. Because of this attitude, they can be gamblers and spendthrift. They tend to believe in keep moving and taking a lot of risks so that they do well in their career whatever they choose.

Moreover, change is their part of life because they get easily bored with the same chores of life. The doors are practical, observant, fun-loving, take action spontaneously, and most essentially try to take out some solution to the problems with their innovative mind.

For the other people, they can be real-time motivators who can change people's mind from a negative aspect from the positive side. The main thing is if they recognize their real talent and try to operate within that realm, then they can accomplish truly exciting things in life personally and professionally.

In the minimum time, they try to fulfill assigned work while finding out a possible solution for that.

The Givers

They have the ability to focus mainly on people, and that's why they are also called people-oriented personality. Sitting alone and doing any work is very difficult for them as they enjoy the company of people. Their people skills are so unique and extraordinary as they have the ability to make people what he/she wants them to do.

The givers get under an individual's skin and are able to get the reaction to what he/she is seeking. Mainly, their motive is unselfish but other people think that they use to manipulate people while using against them.

The givers understand and care about people, and have a special talent to bring the best out of the worst.

Many times, they define their direction according to the people and forget their own motive to do something. This personality is expressive and open, but they are more focused on being responsive and supportive to others.

As they avoid being alone, but they fill the lives of other people while doing various activities which make them happy.

The Mechanic
As the name suggests, they are more inclined towards the way things work. They are good at logic and want to see everything in a practical way. Theories of various experts don't suit the mechanic and they prefer their own way to accomplish things.

Apart from that, their adventurous nature makes them unique from others. That's why they love motorcycles, cars, skydiving, etc. They are more interested in thriving action; as a result, fear is absent in them.

Indeed, no other person can convince them until and unless they have some practical application related to that concept.

Such individuals want to spend their time alone because that time is very beneficial for them to sort things out most clearly. Action-oriented feature in this personality is the most admirable feature which sets them apart from others.

Moreover, they do not believe in systems; rather, they make their own rules and system and follow them with full belief and with the truth.

Notwithstanding, they feel happy when they are centered in action-oriented task inclusive of logics, reasoning, and technical aspects. The mechanics have good hand-eye coordination which makes them very helpful in a crisis. However, they are optimistic, cheerful, loyal to their counterparts, very generous, trusted, and respective individuals who always do the committed work within that time frame.

The Nurturers

Kind-hearted and warm are their most admirable qualities which everyone praises. However, the other person's happiness is more crucial for them than their own interests.

Indeed, their vision is always clear regards to personal or professional life and they know how to attain it. They most value security and kindness and faithfully follow traditions and laws.

They don't want to see the darker side of life and believe in extracting the best out of the worst from people around them. Their thinking is always positive which makes them successful in their life and they only believe people whom they think to be the best.

More so than other types, they are extremely aware of their own internal feelings, and side by side other people's feelings too.

Strong sense of responsibility and duty makes this personality very impressive and unique. Positive feedback is one of the best things they want from others while doing any work; and if in case it is not, then nurturers get discouraged. The nurturers cannot work under stress and if they do, it can be critically wrong.

In their whole life, they can gift many things to people like sensitivity, warmth, generosity, and numerous others.

The Visionary

They are very idealistic people who will see possibilities in every situation. Whatever idea they invent, excitedly they tell everyone about that. As a result, they get the support which is beneficial to attain the goal.

The visionary personality is fluent in conversion, mentally quick, and love to do verbal sparring with people. Great liking for debates makes them very idealists. Their personality is also known as lawyer types who understand every situation faster and logically acts on that situation for the best results.

This personality cannot work under stress; and in case they work, there are chances that they lose their ability to generate possibilities. The most crucial quality of visionary is they value knowledge a lot and spend most of the time in attaining higher understanding.

Furthermore, as they live in a world of possibilities, they get easily towards concepts, challenges, and numerous difficulties which come in their way to achieve anything.

The Inspirers

Inspirers are very talented people who often act as role models for other individuals who want to attain their goal. They are filled with warmth, brightness, enthusiasm, and have the capability to accomplish anything and everything in their life. The way they work in different environments and situations often motivates others to be like them.

Indeed, they want to live their life to the fullest and strive most out of it. Mainly, the inspirer's talents and skills are very broad but they only accomplish those things in which they are interested.

Notwithstanding, this type of personality has great people skills which makes them liked by countless individuals. They have a strong sense of values which ensure dedication towards any relationship.

Basically, inspirers are happy individuals but they get bored with mundane life or you can say strict schedules.

Their best qualities are: -
Charming
Risk-takers
Sensitive
People-oriented who take care of others
Independent

In order to analyze or read people, understanding the other person's personality is extremely useful in maintaining an effective and long-lasting relationship with the other individual. The notion of different personality types is discovered by the experts who explained that an individual is featured into two dimensions, which is further represented by two opposites.

They are sensing versus intuition and thinking versus feelings. Every person contains equally valuable features; which as a result, offers benefit in personal and professional life. If you want to know another person's personality type, describe that individual's qualities. Like: -

Sensing vs. intuition

Sensing people are practical in their approach, but intuition individuals are insightful and irrational

Relies mainly on facts, numbers which are specific. Talking about another part, it relies on insight, theories, and trends of the latest developments

Sensing personality only focus on the present, but intuitions are future-oriented individuals with long-lasting plans

Thinking vs. feelings

Thinking personality is very much governed by rational beginning as compared to feelings which are emotional beginning

Objective, cold, and impersonal are the attributes of thinking individuals but feeling individuals show sympathy, warmth, concern and always support others whatever the situation is

Thinking people use logical analysis and objective methods to solve any issues. Talking with regards to the other category, they find solutions based on gut feelings, good-bad, and likes-dislikes

Extravert vs. introvert

Extravert people use energy which comes from the outside world but introverts are opposite to that

Extroverts like to interact with more people; but, an introvert has few contacts whatever the situation or need is

Extravert personality likes to communicate in a group. Introverts prefer interacting one to one communication

Extraverts don't mind any interruption in their work but the latter one needs a quiet environment to focus

Chapter 4: Critical Rules to Understand People

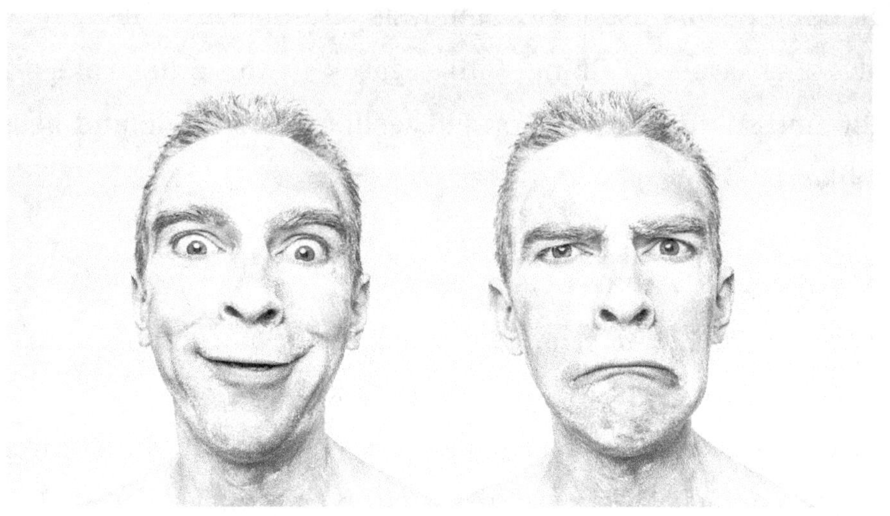

This heading 'critical rules to understand people' might sound overreaching because of the 'rule' word. Human behavior is one of the complex subjects which is very difficult to understand and define. But despite that, still, there are ways to understand different individuals which our experts have found.

Personally, I am also very much interested in what people think, and what excellent ways to manage or fulfill their expectations are. In the whole globe, there are various personalities and understanding each one of them makes no sense, but "impossible" itself says "I am possible."

In our day to day life, we see numerous reactions of an individual which are as natural as the way the wind blows. In this, you are not fully known what to expect and what will be the reaction of another person.

So, the solution to this problem is rather than analyzing each little circumstance, action, and the reaction of human beings; let's understand a little bit about human nature.

People mostly care about themselves

Every human being in this world thinks only about themselves. In this rule, the myth is that people think that other people care or you can say think about us. This doesn't mean that people are selfish or hurtful; rather they just want to focus on themselves most.

Let's talk with an example – out of 100% thoughts, feelings, and emotions, 60% of them are self-directed means you only think about yourself in order to accomplish lifetime focused goals.

My goals, my problems, my feelings, my emotions, etc.

Rest 30% of your concern is in regards to your own relationships which only bothers you. Like what my friends think about me, on what basis my boss will evaluate my performance in the next session, do my friends like my nature or not?

As you are living your social and personal life, you only think about that situation which might occur in your life. So, an individual has no time to understand others feelings and emotions.

Other than this, 10% is left for empathy in which they only think about other individuals' emotions, feelings, perspective, etc. and in this 10%, they divide the ratio between the number of people whom they know. So, you would occupy a small fraction of the percentage in most people's mind.

Individuals have poor memories
For instance, you met one person at a party and while interacting, you have told your name to that person and after some time, he/she forgets it. This is another human behavior rule which is not to be ignored that people have trouble remembering things.

Especially, those data which does not belong to themselves. Nowadays, people are more inclined towards similarities than your differences if you are emotionally attached to them.

Regards to this, it is not essential to remember the person; but if you do, for that you will win credit with small efforts.

People feel lonely

This rule is another broad generalization which is to be taken care of. Nowadays, though having everything people suffer from bouts of loneliness. The application of this rule is that loneliness is fairly common but the thing is if you are feeling alone in a social group, then it might be your own fault.

Every individual is emotional

Numerous people have stronger feelings than they show to the outer world. Individuals who continuously show anger, depression, and many more are generally frowned upon in many cultures.

So, assume everything is fine until and unless someone has a nervous breakdown.

Conformity is the norm

You will actually become in which environment or atmosphere you live. Indeed, your own uniqueness and individuality tend to fit persons in and around you. This rule is also true for another group of people too. So, be careful while picking up your company of friends, colleagues, and a partner.

Means you have control who you want to be.

Chapter 5: What is Personality Development?

All individuals possess certain traits of personality which set us apart from the rest of the world. The mix of good and bad traits tells us how you respond to the situation. According to some studies, it is stated that these traits are genetic and remain fixed throughout life.

But according to some psychologists, they suggest that if you want, you can change these traits for the benefit of self or you can say for people.

So, personality is what makes a person unique and admirable. The personality of an individual consists of several components like temperament, environment, and character. With the help of all these components, you can determine how that person will become or right now is.

Talking regards to temperament, it is a genetic determine factor which shows a person's approach towards the world and how that individual learns about the world. Indeed, there are no genes which are specifically meant for personality, but genes control the nervous system; which as a result, has some effect on human behavior.

Another component called environment is an adaptive pattern related to surrounding of the person in which they live. Some of the psychologists have researched that the first two components that are temperament and environment influence the human personality the most.

Lastly, the third factor called character which is inclusive of emotional, cognitive, and behavioral patterns which are learned through experience determines how a person can think, behave, and feel throughout his life.
Other than this, the character also depends upon our moral values which are inherited in us through our ancestors.

The different stages of life significantly influence personality development, which is a very essential part for the person and the other human beings also. Let's discuss the stages of life: -

Infancy- The first two years of the child are very crucial in which he/she learns basic trust and mistrust. If he/she is well-nurtured and loved by the parents properly, then the infant develops trust, security, and basic optimism. If it is opposite, then the result will be mistrust.
Toddlerhood- It occurs after the first stage starts from three to four years. During this stage, they learn shame and autonomy
Preschool- In this, the child learns initiative and shame. Through active play, they start using imagination, try to

cooperate with others, etc. During this stage, the parents play a very essential role in which they get a restriction on the play and use their imagination.

School-age- In this stage, the whole development of the child takes place in which he/she learns various good habits like teamwork, how to work with rules and regulations, cooperation, and basic intellectual skills. Moreover, self-discipline surges every year with the passing of school age.

If the past stages of the child are excellent, then they learn various good habits otherwise, they feel inferior in front of others.

Adolescence- It is the age between 13 to 14 years in which a child starts behaving like a mature person. The young person starts experimenting new things and if parents are opposed to it, negativity arises. Indeed, this stage starts seeking leadership and rapidly develops a set of ideals for them to live by.

Importance of Personality Development

In order to get success in both personal and professional life, a great overall personality is very crucial in the life of an individual. Every person is automatically influenced by attractive and renowned personality. Whether it is a job, interview, while interacting with other human beings, and many more sectors, you must have certain traits and features which should compel other human beings to say yes! What a great personality!

Nowadays, in every field, the personality of a person matters a lot. For instance- in the interview to impress the interviewer, in business to influence the client and make them believe in you. Therefore, the demand of personality has surged drastically with the passage of time. These days with the advent of personality, every school is careful about it and they make their students a perfect example where they can excel in every field.

Some years ago, the overall concept of personality was very common and no one really approached towards it. Parents also rarely gave importance to it. It was just looking good while wearing good clothes, which is more emphasized in a work-related environment. Indeed, the interviewer just wanted good working skills of the person and not interpersonal skills.
But now the scenario has changed a lot in this age of competition and economic revolution. Let's put some light on the various points of personality which are considered very crucial in personality development: -

Personality development inculcates numerous good qualities
Good qualities can be in any form like punctuality, flexibility, friendly nature, curious about things, patience, eager to help others, etc. However, if you have a good personality, you will

never ever hesitate to share any kind of information with others which benefit them.

According to the rules, you will follow everything like reaching on time at the office. All these personality traits not only benefit you but also to the organization directly or indirectly.

Gives confidence-

Great personality tends to boost your overall confidence. If you know that you are properly groomed and attired, it makes you more anxious towards interacting with people. Other than this- in any of the situation, if you know how to behave, what to say, how to show yourself, then automatically your confidence is on the peak.

Overall, a confident person is liked and praised by everyone both in personal and professional life.

Reduces stress and conflicts-

A good personality with a smile on his face encourages human beings to tackle any hurdle of life. Trust me, flashing a smile on the face will melt half of the problems side by side, evaporating stress and conflicts.

Moreover, with a trillion million smiles on your face, there is no point in cribbing over minor issues and problems which come in the way of success.

Develops a positive attitude-

A positive attitude is that aspect of life which is must to face any hard situation and one to one progress in life. An individual who thinks positive always looks on the brighter side of life and move towards the developmental path. He/she rather than criticizing or cribbing the problem always tries to find out the best possible solution with a positive attitude.

So always remember, if any problem occurs, then take a deep breath-in, stay cool keeping in mind the positivity anyhow. This is because developing a positive attitude in hopeless situations is also part of personality development.

Improves communication skills-

Nowadays, a lot of emphases is given on communication skills as a part of personality development. A good communicator always lives an excellent personal and professional life. Indeed, after your outer personality, the first impression tends to fall on another person is what you say and how you say it.

Verbal communication of the person makes a high impact on another person. Individuals with good communication skills ought to master the art of expressing thoughts and feelings in the most desired way.

Helps you to be credible-

It is a good saying that you cannot judge a book by its cover which also applies to a person. Means people judge a person from their clothing and how it is worn. Therefore, dressing plays a very essential role in the personality of an individual.

So, be careful while picking up clothes for yourself. It doesn't mean you will buy expensive clothes, but they should be perfect and suit your personality.

How to develop a personality

I always used to think that an individual's personality is something which they are born with. Means a bit of nature, a small amount of nurture, and well there you have a bold personality which makes you the center of attraction.

Later in life, I actually considered while seeing people that the fact is a person can change their personality later in life and make it a certain way which eventually looks naturally.

I just want to ask one question from you guys that have you observed any person who is the center of attraction? They have mind-blowing qualities due to which people get attracted to them like a magnet. So, how do they manage to do this?

Actually, they are personified persons who want to learn something or everything to look unique.

The fact is that with the amount of competition you are living with these days to get an excellent job, best spouse, best friend, and everything best- a good personality solves all these issues.

Well, every individual has his own qualities and traits which make them unique. But, some of the tips are very beneficial which help the person to be a perfect example of personality. While making your personality there is no room of age, but the improvement has. It cannot happen in a day, it takes overtime.

So, there are multiple characteristics on which an individual has to work on while developing his personality. Here you will know some tips on developing personality: -

Be a good listener
If a person has good listening skills, they can make another person feel important in front of them, so be a good listener. One of the examples of this is:

Jacqueline Kennedy Onassis was considered one of the adorable women in the whole globe because she enhanced the skill of being an exceptional listener. She was very well-known how she looks into the person's eyes, which make them feel very essential.
This quality is very appealing in order to have an awesome personality.

Take interest in reading and expanding your horizons
The more you gain knowledge about various aspects, the more you become famous in your personal and professional life. So,

read more and cultivate those interests in yourself which make you stand in front of others with confidence.

On the other hand, when you meet people, you have the opportunity to share things with the individuals by making them flat.

Dress up well

While going to the office, party, or on any other occasion, wear dress according to that which suits you. Good looks no doubt add to your personality but what matters is how you dressed up for any occasion. Thus, dressing sense plays a very crucial role in personality development and building confidence.

Observe the body language

While interacting with people, try to use positive gestures which make another person comfortable and relaxed. Some studies stated that 75% of the work is done by verbal communication in which a person's personality is judged by another person.

So, keep an eye on body language.

Remain happy and light-hearted

Try to see the joy in the world and every work that you do. Spend precious and laughing with others so that you feel happy. Always appreciate people in one way or the other. So, smiling and laughing plays a significant role in making your personality awesome.

Stay calm in tensions

Some people have good personality until and unless they come across some tense situation. Don't be that kind of person who becomes angry in tensed issues and shouts on everybody. Therefore, be relaxed and stay cool while finding out the best possible solution for a problem.

Develop leadership qualities

It is believed that good leaders have an excellent personality which can impress another person easily and effectively. However, leadership skills don't mean giving orders to subordinates. Rather, it means how well you can as a leader manage your subordinates to accomplish any task. Indeed, work hard to set an example for them who work with you so that if in the future they will get a chance to work with you, they will feel very excited.

Work on your inner beauty

Most of the people only work on external appearance, but when you behave or speak outside, everything gets reflected. So, it is true that the outer look is essential but inner beauty is also very crucial to be a full-proof personality.

Indeed, it takes only a few days to change your outer appearance but, sometimes it takes years to change the inner world. So, work on that and you yourself can see the difference.

Learn from your mistakes

As a human, mistakes are part of life which makes an actual individual. If you are learning any new thing, you are bound to make mistakes. Always get ready to learn from your mistakes while saying or feeling sorry. Saying sorry will make a significant place to make a respectful corner among your friends or colleagues.

Indeed, if you have made a mistake, forgive yourself and move on.

Always make compliments to others

If you see that someone is looking great or gorgeous, then don't hesitate to say something positive to them. This will make your image or standard up.

Be original

The next essential step in making your personality awesome shows what you actually are. It is a very eminent saying that original is worth than copied things. So, follow this and be how it is; rather, pretending what you are not.

Other than this, one should not copy someone's personality. But, you can adopt some habits of other individuals who are good and help you in developing your personality.

Meet new people with a smile

Try to meet new people which will make you aware of a new environment and culture by which you as an individual can learn new things. Moreover, it also broadens your horizons.

Make your own opinion

The opinion is something which cannot be changed or stolen from another person. For example, while sitting in a group when someone asks your opinion, give them your opinion which is unique and is for the betterment of everyone. This attitude will make you more interested and stimulating to be sociable.

Get out of your comfort zone

Be ready and always get prepared to challenge yourself to learn new skills. Like for most people- learning new things is quite a challenging work. But with a positive attitude and confidence in yourself, you can tackle anything.

Don't give up at any point

Whenever you try to do anything and you fail, then give yourself a second chance to improve it. So, don't give up at any cost and try, try, try until you succeed.

Create your own style

According to my personal experience, you don't need to be a replica of anyone- you need to be yourself.

So, find the best style which makes you comfortable and relaxed. This pattern of developing your personality is very unique which offers the chance to explore and develop over time. Means if you get tired of something, you can move to another style without any downturn.

Be passionate about your work

No one in this world wants to listen to something abrupt regards to their work. In fact, no one is more contagiously attractive than someone who feels passionate and enthusiastic about what they do.

In case you are not happy with your job or work, then don't complain regards to that if you don't have the capability to change the circumstances.

Therefore, figure out your passion and try to make the necessary changes in your life to change the present situation.

Don't make yourself aggressive

Well, in everyday situation there are numerous assertive situations which make you angry. But, be careful because is a big turn off to people, both in social and professional life.

If your nature is like pushy, then be honest to yourself and try to change it as soon as possible.

Don't strive hard for perfection

Keep in mind that you don't have to attain perfection in any field because no one is perfect in this world. When a person is willing to show imperfection, then he/she is putting people at ease.

Evaluate yourself

Evaluation is the best technique to change yourself towards positivity so keep evaluating yourself at regular intervals of time. In this case, take the feedback from your friends, colleagues, and other near and dear ones seriously, which will help you to improve gradually.

Dressing and personality development

In today's competitive world, fashion needs no age or any other types of boundary. Everybody sets his/her own trend in clothing which suits them best and in which they are comfortable. And later on, this own fashion is seen as the latest style which everyone follows.

Whereas, some people want to look simple but trendy but the rest of them might catch the attention and wear something which looks catchy and striking. Whatever the case is, your own clothes style makes a high impact on other people.

The subject of personality development helps the individual in overall development. A person's clothing style plays an essential role in enhancing his or her personality. Other than this, the individuals dressing sense speaks volumes of his/her character and personality.

In order to look different, you really need to know what you are wearing and what you want to wear. Be unique in your dressing style and wear something different. Always see whether the dress you are wearing is suiting your personality or not. Other than this, be careful of your body type, weight, height, and complexion.

Let's some tips which will be very helpful in making your personality awesome: -
First and foremost step comes is dress according to the occasion
Keep in mind whatever you wear should reflect the real you in that dress, means don't overdo it
Never wear tight or body-hugging clothes as they will make you uncomfortable and uneasy
So, craft your whole personality with awesome clothes which depicts you

Here are some tips on how you dress up for an interview: -

General tips-these are the basic hygiene tips which every individual should take care

Your nails should be properly trimmed and manicured

Your hand which shows most of the things about your personality should be clean and unmarked

Keep the pockets of your clothes empty. Means no bulges of a wallet or mobile or coins in the pocket should be seen as it will not create a good impression

Your shoes should be clean and polished

Don't chew gum, or come after smoking before the interview panel

Do not show off your body piercing at any cost

Your hair should be pulled back neatly

Do not wear anything tight or too loose which makes you uncomfortable

Men dressing for the interview

Always wear dark color professional shoes with laces

Keep in mind that your socks should match your trouser

The belt which you will wear should not match with trouser

Men should wear minimum jewelry or no jewelry at all

Wear silk tie with a conservative pattern

Always carry some type of briefcase or portfolio

Use good fragrance for aftershave

Avoid having long beard and mustaches and if you are interested in it, make sure you have trimmed it properly

Clothes should be neat and clean with proper ironing

Color of the suit should be solid

Women dressing for an interview

Make sure you wear a solid color suit which best suits your personality and according to the demands of the profession

Don't wear too much jewelry as it will make a negative impact on the interviewer

Have a neat professional hair cut

Wear sober colored nail polish and it should be neatly applied on the nails

Don't make your ears full of earnings rather, wear only one pair of earnings

Avoid carrying a purse, in fact, carry a briefcase or portfolio for an excellent first impression

Wear only one ring in your hand

At last, I just want to say that the dress you wear reflects your personality and thus it is an essential aspect of an individual's personality. Therefore, make sure what you wear should be neat and tidy and properly ironed.

Indeed, don't pull up your clothes from the wardrobe and wear it for any occasion. Everything has to be in its place according to the need and it should be appropriate according to the place.

You might be thinking that why am I talking about personality development when the book is about reading people and analyzing them. But as discussed earlier, we should develop our own personality first before judging someone else. These points will also help you to figure out how people carry themselves if you know how to do it for your own.

Chapter 6: What are Social Skills?

Social skills are a very crucial part of the personality which helps in making excellent relationships with other individuals. It is used to communicate and interact with each other, both in verbal and non-verbal ways through gestures, body language, and other personal appearance.

In our day to day life, social skills start from saying hello to forging long-lasting relationships. That's why social skills are a very essential part of the human personality.

Let's discuss some of the characteristics of social skills: -

Social skills depend upon the goal which you make for your overall success

Over time it can be learned, taught, and practiced according to the need

Social skills are under cognitive control of the individual which surges with more learning

They can be identified as certain types of behavior whereby on the basis of which individual can be judged and categorized

They are interrelated in the sense that one person may use more than one kind of behavior at the same time

It should be appropriate to the situation where and when it is used

Italians are considered as very social and outgoing because they emphasize much on communication and both personal professional relationships and its part of the reason that they have a reputation for conveying warmth and openness with both natives and non-natives, alike.

So, you also can make your own reputation by adapting social skills which is a part of personality development.

In turn, let's put some light on the advantages associated with having good social skills:

You can increase your relationships
The better you are in living in relationships, your success will drastically improve. So, focus on your relationships whether it

is personal or professional like landing in a better job, can make new friends, and give you a better outlook in life.

Improves communication skills

The more you interact with people in a group, one to one, and many more can rapidly improve the communication level. However, you cannot avail good social skills without having amazing communication skills. This is because, with the help of these skills, you can openly convey your thoughts and ideas to the people.

Create more efficiency

In this regard, if you are good at people, you cannot avoid being with people at any cost. For example, in the business get together, you want to spend time with anyone regards to finalizing some deal but he/she can't help to choose a particular deal. At this point intime, your social skills will work which allow you to politely convey the message that you want to spend some time with other folks.

Gives you a chance for a better career

The most lucrative jobs often involve a large amount of time spent while interacting with employees, media, and colleagues. It is a very rare case that particular individuals strict to their office and excel in every field. Nowadays, every company looks for people who have particular tactical skills, which means the ability to work in a team and influence and motivate others to get things alone.

Help in surging overall happiness

Getting along with people, while understanding them will help you to open personal and career-related goals. However, striking up a conversation at the work-related place may lead to delivering a higher salary and a simple smile on your face which can also help grab a new partner.

It is also observed that retired persons with large social skills have a higher amount of happiness as compared to others.

Types of social skills

The reasons for social skill deficit in an individual can be innumerable which makes the person on backtrack. It could occur because of the lack of knowledge in various sectors, but it can be improved. Sometimes, in many cases, people know the social skills but lack of inadequate practice and feedback takes the individual on the back foot. So, there are numerous internal and external things that interfere with the person performing the social skills. Here you will come to know the types of social skills: -

Basic communication skills

This type of communication skill is inclusive of the ability to listen, refrain from speaking, and follow the directions accurately. The social skills ability to listen to include concentration while ignoring distraction. The best sign of good listening skills is attention on what someone is saying such as nodding and smiling, and on the other hand, delivering feedback on what is said.

Moreover, good communication also includes language and body languages like eye contact with the person, physical stillness, and emotional attentiveness when another individual is speaking.

Empathy and rapport skills

There are certain cognitive, behavioral, and mental health conditions which limit one individual to feel empathy side by side connecting with others. Those persons who suffer from severe social anxiety and others who are very self-conscious can display very little or too much focus on someone else.

This means that most of the people with this anxiety are very desperate to please others while taking care of what they speak or they always help others.

And the opposite people will feel overwhelmed by social interaction and keep away from every individual.

Interpersonal skills

Interpersonal skills are a very essential part of social skills which includes the capability of sharing things with others, asking for permission from someone, waiting for turns, and numerous others. Those individuals who have limited social skills hesitate to ask or share anything. Moreover, adults may struggle to understand proper manners in varied context and settings.

The skill of problem-solving

This skill needs a problem-solving attitude on the side of the person. It can be in the form of asking help from others, saying sorry in case you have done some mistake, coming on conclusion quickly, and accepting consequences which come in your life. Most of the individuals struggle to identify the root causes of problems, and that's why they are not able to understand potential solutions.

Indeed, those persons who struggle to identify the solution of any of the issues have an introvert personality. They always prefer to avoid problems because it makes them uncomfortable and uneasy.

Accountability

Some of the individuals are very petrified if they get criticism in public. Those persons are not able to accept the blames, while dealing with constructive feedback. Accountability is also an essential part of conflict management as it is recognizing mistakes is an excellent way to signify conciliatorily and cooperate attitude.

So, those persons who want to improve their social skills should focus on imitating desirable attitude and can work towards unwanted behavior. Furthermore, there are various options by which a person can improve their social skills in an effective way.

Are social skills essential for success?

In our school life or you can say in college while studying academics, our professors have taught us how to read a book, how to answer any question, how to improve your writing and various others. Do you remember any teacher telling you how to interact with others, how to cope up with conflicts; deal with your emotions, No! Have you thought regards to it?

But in these types of situations, the real secret of success underlies which you will come to know by experience or when someone tells you things in regard to this. It's not at all about having expertise in your field; but, the secret of success goes beyond the goal- achievement attribute.

These days rarely any person will know what social skills are and why they are crucial for success. In order to get this answer, you will get the best social media rules because everyone is busy on social media. Nowadays, countless individual spends most of their fixated time on social media ignoring the most essential elements of being social.

However, when you rewind your clock some years before, you will come to know the proper techniques and practices which are best to develop social skills in a person.

When a business reaches its ultimate height- the businessman, managers, other C, and D level employees forgot the impact of correct use of social skills in their personal and professional life. This offer ugly results, and loss in business, not having customers, and not getting any opportunity to excel their business.

That's why social skills are a very much contributing factor in getting success in both personal and professional life. This is not which you want to gain just to improve your personal and professional relationships. These are soft skills that you need in order to become successful in your career. The good news is that it can be learned with proper practice.

So, if you are not getting along with people, having a lack of social skills can be the most essential reason for that. However, in everyone's life, there are people with whom you want to interact in order to continue living. Therefore, if you will not find common ground with others you will lose the grip from your job, from business, or in personal life as well.

According to the Stanford social innovation review, just like 20 years old boy/girl develops fluent language skills through training and practice like that social competencies can be learned and developed with practice.

Let's guide yourself how to hone your social skills which are a must to be a good employee, best businessman, effective in personal life, and innumerable others to touch the heights of success.

Be a good listener

Don't just listen to what another person is saying, rather be an active listener. It means being fully engaged when someone is talking with you. There are many useful things which you have to keep in mind while listening like- create eye contact, nod the head when you agree with something, and also you can ask questions in order to clarify.

The first and foremost thing which as a listener you have to keep in mind is don't interrupt the person when he/she is saying something. This is also a token for respect. Well, when you get used to listening to people like this, you automatically see your positive side.

Cooperation

Teamwork is very crucial in an organization to attain a common goal. Therefore, it is very important for the individual to understand his role and responsibilities in order to be successful otherwise it will impact the overall progress of the project.

For this reason, make sure that every team member including you makes every possible effort to complete the project in time. And in case any team member needs your help, then you are ready to do that.

Behave in a disciplined manner

According to the rules and regulations of the organization or you can say at home also, always behave in a disciplined manner. Being disciplined means behaving in a manner that aligns with a set of norms, customs, laws, policies, and any other guidelines. Sometimes these norms are imposed or socially acceptable to make the workplace a better place to live. Indeed, if a person is disciplined, he/she voluntarily complywith the rules of a particular environment. This, as a result, shows self-control and which on the other hand other members of the team easily accept it.

Always select an effective way of communication

This is very essential if you want to learn and practice social skills. Indeed, there are numerous ways by which you can communicate with your colleagues, friends, or your boss. Ensure that you are adopting the right channel for communication.

For example: Don't discuss your issues via email, chat, and or by phone call. Because in these electronic media, there are no emotions, feelings, or empathy and you are opening a can of worms towards you.

Even though, the wrong usage of a comma can change the meaning of a full sentence. So, be careful while communicating with another person and choose the right medium of communicating.

Show respect to others

It is a nice proverb-" Give Respect and Take Respect." No matter what position you are sitting, showing respect to others is a sign of regard. When you are giving respect, it means on your behalf you are caring, admiring, and honoring their position.

Moreover, never ever feel that I am better than anyone in terms of position, experience, and knowledge. Keep in mind that staying humble with others while being mindful is a great social skill which everyone will like to possess.

Think positive and be positive

There is a high connection with being positive and a positive attitude. The individuals who think positive remains the center of attraction every time because, with a positive attitude, they can solve every problem which comes in their life.

However, there is nothing that in the lives of positive people ups and downs are not there, but they effectively and with a positive attitude figure out everything and don't wallow in self-pity, doubt, and negativity.

Empathy

It is also an important skill in terms of socializing which means having good relation with another person while understanding them. However, if as a good human being if you listen to other people's concerns and feelings and put yourself in their shoes, you can really understand them perfectly.

In this way, with the help of empathy, you can generate better solutions to issues because you already know that what another person thinks, need, and want.

Furthermore, don't forget that treat others like the way you want to be treated. Through this way, you can bring a positive return from another person and which also help you to read people's mind.

Patience

The countless number of frustrations as a person we encounter are related to other persons in the form of traffic jams, delay in work, disruptive noise around us. These things are very common every now and then and occur everywhere.

I want to ask one question regards to this- can they be avoided?

Indeed, sometimes they may be avoided but ultimately it can result in frustration. So, the solution to this problem instead of playing the game of guilt party, relax and try not to take any tension without bothering people. Be patient.

Forgiving

When any person has done the mistake, which is very serious and is unforgiving, then also you forgive that person without taking it personally. It is that right attitude that you are learning and practicing social skills.

Moreover, always keep in mind that resentment deprives us of opportunities to deepen the relationships while connecting in a positive way in and around us.

The foremost step in social skills is being human

If you want to be unique and admirable, then, first of all, you have to be human. People will like you for you, not for anyone else. That doesn't mean you offer arrogance, brash, and unwilling to compromise; rather, be flexible, happy, and positive.

So, be the best of you so that other individuals will want to be around you and share you with the world.

The list of above social skills may seem like common sense, but it is very surprising that these uncommon senses are affecting most of the workplaces today.

Other than this, social skills are also very helpful in reading people's mind or analyzing them in order to understand them easily and effectively.

The best part of these social skills is that they are very useful in converting the environment of the workplace into positive and effective; which as a result, assures better production.

How to learn social skills?

Good social skills are an essential part of building excellent relationships, enjoying yourself in public, help in analyzing people, and the best part is you will get success in life.

However, if you feel awkward while attending any social events or struggle in entering any conversation which will, in turn, affect your social life and your career. So, in order to read people and set up your own life, these social skills will help you to do so in an effective manner.

Behave like a social person

Be social in front of the other social creatures, even if you don't like. So, don't allow anxiety to hold your back and make a hard decision to talk to enter into conversations.

However, with time, it will get easier and you will quickly improve social skills. Side by side if you are able to understand others then only you will be able to read their minds.

Be aware of the volume and the tone of your voice

While in a conversation, don't speak too softly or too loudly either. Speak at that volume which is heard by everyone easily, and shows confidence, not aggression.

Keep in mind to adjust the volume of your voice according to the surrounding environment

If it is possible, try to speak at that volume in which everyone is speaking

In case you speak fast, then slow down your volume it is called as normal speed. This type of talk will make you speak slowly which help you to speak clearly and effectively

Always make yourself interested in people's stories

In this regard, we are a bit inorganic that's why we love people who are interested in our stories. So, be interested in them and they will be interested in you.

Just observe other people how they behave in social situations

In order to analyze people closely, watch their body language and consider what are the essential points at which they are good at socializing. Moreover, observe their postures, gestures, facial expressions, and eye contact. These things will ultimately improve your social skills and also help in analyzing people.

Furthermore, determine how well the people are observing when you know each other. This part is very crucial because the body language shared by one person to another may differ which will also help you to read people.

Always talk to that person who seems interested, not busy

Always approach this individual with an open mind and language which shows that you are interested in knowing each other. This opportunity will offer you a chance of meaningful conversation while analyzing each other.

Keep these things in mind when you approach any person: -
Be confident while reaching any person
If you are nervous, then it will make another person hesitate while talking to you
Always remember to put away your mobile phone aside as it will annoy some individuals while talking
Listen to the other person's opinion regards to any topic so that it will help you to judge that person, and side by side promote self-learning.

Know when to leave

By the way, don't get me wrong, but nobody wants to chat with you for hours. So, take your time and leave the place if you want that another person will not get bored with you.

It's all about love

Love is the key ingredient of all problems if you want to solve it. That is an ultimate social trick. So, love people, respect them, admire persons, compliment others, try not to judge people, forgive them at any cost, and do numerous other things which show love towards them as a good human being.

Spend some time with yourself while getting ready

When you get ready smartly, then automatically confidence comes in you which as a result make all other social issues easier. So, develop a routine which makes you self-confident and more social. Other than this, being able to analyze yourself makes you read others as well.

Excellent social skills are also very crucial in analyzing people and make you the best in speed-reading people. So, adopt these techniques of socializing and watch what the other person will think with regards to the situation and people.

Chapter 7: How to Interpret Verbal Communication?

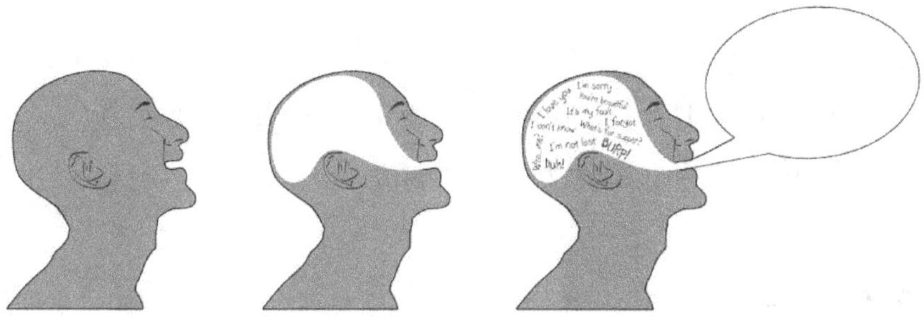

Almost every job all over the globe needs verbal communication skills. That's why it is ranked number 1 on candidate evaluation checklist used by numerous interviewers. Nowadays, stronger your verbal communication skills higher the chances of getting hired regardless of the job for which you are applying.

So, as a candidate, you have to give your best to flatten the interview broad by your verbal communication skills.

Now, the question arises- What is verbal communication?

It is more than just speaking or talking. Verbal communication is all about passing any type of information from one person to another in an effective way. In this, both the speaker and the listener are equally important.

Verbal communication is a soft skill and very much essential for the employer. The workforce which conveys their messages clearly and effectively are highly valued by an organization.

Employees who are good workers as well as who can interpret messages and act according to what they have received have higher chances of excelling in their job.

Moreover, the effectiveness of verbal communication variably depends upon the tone of the speaker, clarity of speech, volume, speed, body language, and words in which he/she choose to interpret. In this verbal communication, there is simultaneous feedback because of one to one conversation.

Talking about the speech, the speaker must keep his tone while the conversation is loud so that it is easily audible keeping the audience in mind. On the other hand, in verbal communication, the speaker has to cross-check whether the message has been understood by the opposite person or not. This communication is prone to errors because sometimes words are not sufficient to express the feelings and emotions of the person.

Importance of verbal communication:

Mainly, verbal communication is considered in the corporate world which is the key to maintain business relationships. If the verbal communication is effective then only it can automatically surge productivity, reduce a smaller number of errors, and at last boosts the relationships in a better way.

First and foremost comes is the image of the organization which is portrayed by the way employees communicate with each other. The customer or client after watching this will judge the standard of the company which is also called first or last impression

Excellent verbal communication skills of the employees of the company help in fostering superb relationship among customers, clients, and various organizations

Indeed, if the communication level between employee and employer is outstanding, then the satisfaction level also boosts

When the communication is effective between the workforce, then they feel secure in the company which as a result enhances confidence and productivity

Other than this, if the communication level is good then the ability of an individual to share ideas, thoughts, and concerns also increases which will further impact the company as a whole

The marvelous thing is it reduces the cultural and language differences in the company as everyone comes from diverse backgrounds.

How to improve verbal communication?

Sublime verbal communication skills are the demand of today which candidates have to clear at any cost. The reason behind this is nowadays, it is very essential to understand and to be understood by both the listener and the speaker to get successful. Moreover, if you want a thriving career, it is very crucial to have superlative verbal communication skills which also help a person to analyze people.

Let's come up with some secrets which will help the youngsters to get excellent verbal communication: -

Read as much as you can

Reading is a very good habit which improves the vocabulary and also helps you to express your ideas more effectively and clearly. As well as, it is very useful in choosing the right words which can impress the other individual.

However, it also eliminates weaknesses in your language skills. Moreover, if a person will read books according to their field, then the knowledge also surges.

Reinforcement

Reinforcement is a very good technique in which there is the use of encouraging words along with non-verbal gestures like, head nod, a smile on the face, warm facial expressions, and eye contact.

This will create rapport and also generates openness in others. The benefits of reinforcement are:

Motivate the other individual to participate in debates or discussions; which as a result, boosts confidence

Clear the way of development
Individual improves the habit of shyness and nervousness when he/she speaks in front of others
Maintain good relationship with colleagues and the employer
Motivate the other individual to participate in debates or discussions; which as a result, boosts confidence

Listen carefully

In the corporate world, listening more and talking less proves to be a very effective tool to build a strong rapport. This will help people to trust you and show that you understand their needs or wants.

Most importantly, make eye contact with that person to whom you are listening so that he/she may feel special.

Prepare yourself for any of the situations

If you see that you are going to anticipate any situation, then prepare the answers to the questions which you may think that can be asked. For example, you have to deliver a presentation so regards to that topic, prepare a format of tricky questions and answer so that it will be easy for you to give the correct answer.

Summarizing

Summarizing is just the overview of main points which has been told by which you will recapitulate the whole concept. This trick is the best verbal communication skill by which both the parties agree to the message and make sure that the communication is effective.

Be mindful

To have a healthy conversation or interaction make sure, that it is full of words, tone, gestures, facial expressions, and body language so that it will go with the conversation.

However, it is vital to remember that communication, whether it is verbal or non-verbal, is made up of the sum of its parts. Researchers suggest that the verbal element in communication is a very small part of the overall message around 20-30%. Then also it is a very significant part of the corporate world.

So, pack up your bags and improve your verbal skills and side by side after mastering on it analyze people in order to understand them.

Chapter 8: What is the Importance of Talking?

Talking is something without which life would not be easy, isn't it? What actually is talking?

Technically it is the exchange of thoughts or opinions or emotions in spoken or sign language. It doesn't need to be in spoken or sign language always, it can be in writing or expression or symbols.

Elementarily talking is the technique of sharing one's feelings and communicating with others. It would not be apt to say that life without talking is impossible as deaf to survives. But they too talk with signs. All living beings interact and express themselves in their own languages of sound.

Do you know animals to talk? Millions of thanks to the man who initiated talks as in its absence, people will feel alone despite being in a group. The life on the globe would go in depression and many may suffer more health hazards if they do not express themselves.

Talking should not be hurting rather it should be pacifying, polite and chivalrous. Your talks can give wounds deeper than a weapon at the same time talking technique should not be unimpressive. Talking is important and plays a significant role in the success and peace of professional as well as social life. Have a look at underneath to know, how you should be talking in general when you meet a stranger for the very first time.

How to talk

Before telling you about the techniques to talk, I would like to tell you a little about positive Body Language. Body language speaks a lot about you, your character, personality, in fact, can reveal inside out of your whole persona. Along with talking, one needs to work on his body language too. Just go through the points below to impress the other person with your body language too along with imbibing to engaging talks.

Smile

Have a million-dollar smile on your face. While having conversations, have a check on your body language too along with the words you utter. To approach with the smile is one way that can aid you winning half of the battle. A smile can be damn effective. Offer a smile first when you have eye contact with the other person. It is a great way to connect with a stranger or someone not well known. Give a quirky smile not cunning. Your body should be in support of a smile. No matter how finely you smile, the other person will in a fraction of second grasp your fake smile and the formality behind it on giving smile not assisted well by your body.

Smiling is also an effectual approach to signify your interest and support. If anyone in a party or one of your co-workers stop beside you, your smile would be a welcoming gesture to initiate talks or at least a sign of being noticed.

Make eye contact

Eye contact reveals your confidence as well as interest while chatting, therefore is extremely important to look into the eyes of others. It is a clear demonstration of your engagement with the other person. It shows that you are listening and respectful to the other person's opinion. The eye is a reflection of emotions like annoyance, affection, boredom, suspicion, etc. You can easily gauge the reaction of the other person by peeping into his/her eyes.

Do blink your eyes while talking or else it will be counted as staring. Staring is a wrong gesture that reflects some chary intentions. Just focus on his eyes and do not look at his/her body upside down or vice versa. If you do so, the other person may get up and walk off and never talk to you again. You can gaze naturally on surrounding while talking, but remember maximum talks done should be with eye contact.

Nod your head

Nod your head while talking as it is an effectual means for nonverbal cues that can be used to express your interest and consent on the ongoing topic of the conversation. It is an indication of the fact that you are getting what the other person is saying. Nodding signifies your support in addition to approval mentioned earlier. Continuous nodding is to be avoided along with bobble-head as this undo the credibility of gesticulation of nodding.

Build your confidence

Your body language often reveals anxiety and state of your well-being. If you are shy, it can be nerve-racking to talk to people. The finest mode to inculcate confidence in you for a conversation is preparing yourself for many scenarios or situation. For instance, if you are supposed to meet a few people at a social get together or meet clients in a corporate get together, prepare some topics as per the occasion. You cannot talk about dresses on corporate events and vice-a-versa. Topics must be general and interesting in meeting a stranger. Avoid cheesy or flattering topics along with making personal comments.

Rehearse conversation to sharpen your skills. Face up to you to converse to someone new each day belongs to different profession and background. It can be a stranger on the street or someone in your neighbor.

Confidence is a key not only on social and professional front but is must while approaching a romantic interest. On finding an opening line, try it on the person you are romantically inclined to without a hitch and hesitation.

How to talk to a new person?

Often, we find it hard to initiate the talk and this turns out to be more draining when you sit opposite to a person not known or just know him by a face like many working for your company. The toughest aspect of it is when you think of starting the conversation with them. Try to find some ground to gear up the talking pace with the stranger you have not met at all.

Don't give a kick start to your talk by using sentences about the weather and all as it looks clumsy and the stranger may find you lumbering. Try to give your introduction and then a general comment to start with a smirk on your face. You can continue further on getting a response in a pleasing tone.

Another topic to start your talk is to give a positive remark on the individual you like to talk to. You could comment that you loved her bag or accessory.

Choose the Right Person to Approach

There is also the right time to start the conversation with and check that he or she isn't too busy to talk. While marching towards him, try to make eye contact with him and if you get a friendly reaction from him, go on to shake hand and high to him. If someone is already speaking to someone else, just refrain yourself from incepting the conversation with him. At parties, you can start the talk with something like "that dip is must to taste" or why not to offer a drink.

Wherever you are, just confirm that you are approaching the right person and that individual is not already busy with something else.

Plan a meeting with someone you know

If you want to talk to a person you have met already but don't know how to start, put up a question to him. Questions are a great means to initiate the talks and you may ask about last weekend or talk about your common office if you both are colleagues.

Keep it simple

Don't be loud and try to start with a few simple and obvious words. It is not like a speech in your school or college where opening lines often decides the fortune of participants. Start with Hi or how are you but remember a smile is not be compromised for talk. The other person will talk and will respond with a reply to your Hi. By keeping things simple, you can start the conversation and permit the person to get started. It will also help you to feel relieved from pressure.

Avoid oversharing

Whether you are meeting the person for the first time or have met him earlier, avoid oversharing on being not really friendly with him. You may be at the risk of over-sharing if you are habitual of gibbering.One should avoid oversharing until and unless they are the one in your list of close folks. One should restrict himself from unfolding the sensitive and private information with the lesser-known folks.

They may not be interested or could be uncomfortable in knowing your personal matters. People usually get irritated with over-friendly and over-sharing folks. The other guy may end up the conversation with an excuse of a busy schedule or some other false excuse. While talking, simply do not talk about too personal and irrelevant matters.

Choose the appropriate time to talk

Silence should not always be filled with the sounds of chit-chatting. But there is a time when one should also stay silent. Is the person sitting next to you too is busy in his official work or he is disinterested in making eye contact with you, just don't make the mistake of talking to him. If someone is taking a small nap while traveling or relaxing after a hectic day with headphones on, just let him chill and dare not to interrupt him.

After initiating the talks, check out how to maintain the flow of Dialogue

Go on to ask questions

It is vital that silence does not intervene after an exchange of a few dialogues. Once you have given the kick start, you got to do many things to make it interesting as well as maintain the tempo of talk. Putting questions is quite an effectual means to keep the talks going. Try to ask small favors which should not be monetary at all. Some pieces of advice from the person will result in dual benefits. One you will get tips and secondly the person with you will offer tips happily which will, in turn, help you in keeping the conversation going.

Go for open-ended questions

Do not ask questions that will be answered in only yes or no. Ask open-ended questions to keep the flow of chat going. Like instead of asking how your health is? Ask I remember you were on sick leaves. What happened and got to know later on that you were hospitalized too. You have really become weak due to sickness etc. Or instead of asking how was your trip? Ask him where did you go? Is it right to visit that place in peak season or when is the right time to visit that place.

You can also convert your question into compliments like I like your blazer. "How do you find such smart pieces"

Honesty is the best policy

Don't just force talk. Chat about the topics that generally interests you and off course you care about.The other person will easily get an idea of your show off. If you think you can fool the other person and become smart, then do not underestimate others. Everyone is smart to read your mind and heart through various modes. Maintain the element of honesty in your conversation to keep the person inclined to chat.

Avoid conversation killers

The degree of comfort gradually increases as time passes while talking. But you need to make constant efforts to keep up the conversation flow. Remember do not include those topics that could embarrass or humiliate the other person. Work on making the other individual comfortable instead. Do not make your talk boring by involving boring individuals into it and also avoid chatting on boring topics that could create boredom and could result atthe end of chat too. Don't talk about rugby, if he hardly knows about the sport or about a favorite reality show in which he shows complete disinterest. Give chance to others to be part of the conversation and speak out.

Thump with the right tone and small talks are that is needed to keep the other person involved. Unnecessarily stretched topics will make the other person lose interest. People get attracted and impressed with positive folks usually. Be positive and do not talk negatively about anything. While being in some kind of doubt, try to mention something upbeat.

It's fine to empathize about a scratchy situation and to resolve it simply try to put a constructive spin on it.

Shuffle topics-

Talking cannot be continued for hours and hours on one topic. Stay ready to move on to other question other than the question of ice breaking.Best way to be prepared to pay attention is to be versed with current events and culture. Talking about movies, sports,
other as this will keep the conversation flow look natural.

Involve more people

Reach out to more folks in your conversation. More people you involve in talks, lesser would be the pressure of talks on you. Invite others to join in a manner that the other person does not get an impression of your state. Involving others to your talk would be a portrayal of traits of your personality as well along with letting the pace of talks unhampered.

Be a good listener

As discussed in the earlier part of the book,Listening is vital. Practice listening to become a proficient conversationalist. Listening is no less important than talking. One can signify his engagement in talk through listening and body language.

Involve neutral statement like "Great" or "that's amazing." To encourage the story of the other person, give comments, "go on please, I simply love it."

Chapter 9: How to Win Friends and Influence People

What would be the meaning of success, if you do not have friends to celebrate the moment of pride and achievement with you? For the moments of bliss as well as grief, one should have friends but in today's time, it is genuinely hard job to have some friends of same age group. Reason being a complex lifestyle, cut-throat competition, Self- centered approach and many more. But still, amongst these odds, there are few lucky guys surrounded by friends and havingan influence on almost everyone knew or strangers to them.

If you fantasize to have an influential personality with real friends all around, learn the know-how to deal with people and techniques to bring the element of comfort with them to make the life a beautiful journey.

To understand the need of having an impressive personality and companion, I would like to narrate an anecdote which is true and was experienced by a near and dear one of mine. Whether it is a report card of any grade of school or college or the spellbinding contentment of passing out with great grades, we want to share it with each and everyone around us. Likewise, the smirk of fetching the first job even before passing out was too valuable and this guy wanted to tell everyone and eventually impress. Despite being the smartest of all in his classroom, had literally nobody impressed and appreciating him. The truth was disheartening and the journey of school ended with no friends by him.

Joined his job and the tale was no different. Once during a meet with higher officials of his concern, he objected to the proposal and pointed it out. He felt that by expressing his point of view fearlessly has proved his intelligence and superiority over others at the meet, but soon learned that he was not effective in handling the people.

During get together, breaks and hang out, he would talk about himself like his life, plans, likes, dislikes with sparing no time for others to utter more than just a few words.

After a year, he was fired from the job and he still couldn't understand the reason and felt that it was the company's loss.

Do you know despite being a scholar and an efficient employee what was wrong with this guy?

Hewas a disappointment with talking about his behavior in terms of human relationship.He was absolutely on the wrong side of the river. He was least bothered about things going on in the life of his colleagues, had no words of appreciation from himself or precisely he was interested in himself only.

To be liked by someone you have to like others, to be the center of interest of others you got to show interest in their lives too and you got to spend time on them to make them spare some time for you.

Can you fall for someone who is least interested in knowing you and bear have no importance in his life?
I bring you some guidelines for the folks on how to be liked by people around and how to win their camaraderie.

KEY POINTS

Develop genuine interest in people around you

Key to the heart of a friend is interest in him. Generate genuine interest in them and believe me this will work unexpectedly. But don't forget do not show unreasonable interest. Unreasonable interest in the lives of people may land you in soup and you may earn criticism as well as isolation. Everyone down the line is self-centered but we don't dwell in an isolated island. You may run in the need of friends sooner or later. This guy would not have suffered had he shown genuine interest in his schoolmates, college mates, and colleagues.

Be a Good Listener

Take some time out of your busy schedule to listen to others. The purpose behind having a mouth and two ears are that you need to listen more to others than speak. One should be a good listener and motivate others to express themselves.

Be a great listener and pay full attention to the folks on the other side. Show them that you are interested in the events of your life. Your happiness matters the most and so does your tears. Have a twinkle in your eye and dance in joy when they feel happy.

If you want to bag friends, you have no choice but to listen to them as people are interested in themselves more and they are topic of chat, than what others have to talk about. People will consider you as a great raconteur if you pay attention to them. A great communicator is one who does not interrupt the others flow of talk and listen.

Talk about their interests, not yours

Talking about the interest of people is a key to win their hearts. Talk about their family, their health, professional life, and personal life only if they are comfortable. Let them go on and on while talking about themselves. This will develop a sort of likeness for you. In this case, you will experience what they have experienced or in other words, you tour the whole journey with them. Every moment you get to learn something and who knows, you too may get answers to some unanswered questions of your life.

Make them Feel Important

Every human being wants an important place in the lives of known ones and want to be appreciated. If you like to occupy an important place in their jaunty of life, you too have to give priority as well as the importance to them. Similarly, to be appreciated, try first to appreciate others.

You must have heard a law that every action has an equal and opposite reaction. It is applicable in this case too. The more importance you give, higher would be the degree of importance offered to you.

Arouse in Them an Eager Want

All of us dream of the things that we want to obtain and this is the reason that we do things to accomplish our dreams or wants. However, not all turn lucky and attain the things they genuinely want to attain. It caters an opportunity to let people fall under your influence by helping others to attain what they aspire for. Such an individual who can arouse the desire or eagerness in other folks will always have a true companion or would never have to be alone.

To generate the urge in people, first of all, try to know what they desire. Analyze from their perspective followed by implication of your perspective to have a better idea and insight of their wants and what can be a motivating tool for them. Have a detailed discussion with them and provide your guidance eventually to help them to attain their aim. If you succeed in convincing them about the solution that you store for them, they will try or initiate to build a connection with them.

For instance, you may have been trying hard to convince your father or brother to quit smoking or alcohol or just sweets. All efforts must have been in vain, no matter how logical your reasons would be. In such a situation, we do not forget to show them the latest articles and blogs having insight into the deadly impacts of their addiction.

In an instance, a daughter said to her addicted father that don't you want to do trekking and sky walking with me. She expressed her desire to roam all around the world and witness different landforms on the globe. The father amazed and inspired with the idea of traveling, determined to give up his addiction and started to follow a fitness regime to become fit for the tour as he dreamt of such a tour secretly.

The only line of attack through which you can encourage anyone to do anything is by providing them the things they want. So, it is advised to know the people's desire and stimulate their urge to get them under your influence.

Keep away from Arguments
Arguments are that we all want to top on, but the fact is that nobody wins them. Defensiveness erupts in the argument,

everyone safeguards their perception. Everyone confirms to win the argument, but nobody actually wins in and mostly gives rise to quarrels and disputes. We all want to win arguments, however, no one wins in such. Do not pre assume that you have won the argument if you think so then you are mistaken?

Analyze the common points between others and yourself and work out on the things that both of you can give consent a . Instead of keeping the argument on, try to listen to them first and understand their point of view. Honesty and calmness are that you need to maintain so that you can accept the fact and always listen first and get their point of view. Do not be in haste to conclude; often the decision taken in anger turns out to be a disaster. The solution to a dispute is giving time to the folks involved. If the other party gives you time to thank then just thank them.

Be grateful to your rival. Agree with the people to melt their confrontation.

Solutions to any argument are simply avoiding it or just give your consent to it to stop heat up. The more you resist people, the more they would dig in. Agreeing doesn't mean that you are giving up or you lost. Those who maintain tranquility actually win and influence people around for the long term.

Respect them or respect their Opinions

Respect can aid you to resolve matters with any degree of complexity. Pay respect to opinion of another side even though they do not agree with you. Being respectful to others can help you to earn their respect and seek out the solution. Even though there is some dispute between you and your friend, do not go to the extreme and scold him with foul language, boorish gestures, high pitch tone, and antagonistic looks. If you do, you may lose their friendship for forever as no one can forgive disgraceful behavior from the other end.

It is human tendency to revert to threats. The scope of settlement diminishes completely, more you threaten the other and they would strike you back from the front or behind secretly. If you like to opt for settlement be courteous to the other person.

Confess your fault or slip up

Confession not only brings an end to argument but also generates the feeling of respect and sympathy within your opponent. I would suggest do not defend you as fools do it. It initiates the positivity of graciousness and ecstasy within the opponent.

Do not delay in accepting your mistake. It becomes highly important when the other person or people involved are well aware of the blunder. In case if you do not accept your mistake, it may hamper your image and you may be called as critical, cynical and narrow-minded. By criticizing yourself and expressing your fault, you can expect forgiveness, support, and understanding from them.

Implement it prior to the things get really bad and you lose the relationship.

Be a Friend

Abraham Lincoln once quoted that "A drop of honey catches more flies than a gallon of gall."

Initially, on meeting an individual for the very first time, try to be friendly. Do not get over-friendly as most of the folks consider them as a chatterbox. People usually get comfortable as well as attracted to people with warmth, welcoming, friendly and approachable attitude. On the contrary, we usually become reserved when we meet introvert, cold and less speaking individual.

If you want others to respond to you just in the manner you want, be friendly towards them. It is a human tendency to revert in the way one usually gets the treatment. By being friendly, one can prove to be a better influencer.

Let Them Do a Lot of the Talking

Let them reveal their grievance or complaints and do not interrupt in the meantime. It is normal as it is hard to please everyone and be perfect. In case of business especially, you are bound to face complaints. Spare time to sit and listen with patience and control on yourself. Understand and know the root cause of it to be able to provide a solution to it.

Just like arguments, try to settle complaints too.

Step in their shoes or see things from their eyes

It is perhaps the hardest of all to do.

The great Abraham Lincoln once said that he spent more time thinking about other people and less time on what he wanted to hear. If you want to be successful, you need to comprehend their viewpoint first. Replace yourself and live their life for a moment and then decide whether they are right or not. Whenever you are asking something from anyone, take a breath and a break followed by putting the question to yourself: why would he want to do it. You will realize that everyone is sailing in the same boat and has almost similar perception and emotions.

Give Your Sympathy

Avoid playing the blame game. To procure mutual aid from others, avoid blaming them for anything. Express your sympathy on finding them bit irrational, annoying and dogmatic. They would not only appreciate but fall in love with you. They may even express their apologies.

If they come off to you as annoying, bigoted, or unreasonable, give them your sympathy instead. They will love you for that. They might even apologize.

In place of orders, put up questions

In today's time, even a subordinate hates to get orders, though they do not have a choice but to listen to their boss. The situation is just the same when   we talk about friends. Ask questions to them and avoid giving instructions or orders. A feeling of comfort, friendliness, and respect to others, aids in gaining the confidence of friends and colleagues along with generating the feeling of being important.

Let us have an answer to the question raised in the effectiveness of this principle -
The other person feels respected as well as important.
It doesn't let the pride of people get hurt.
 Feeling of slaves does not trouble

People greatly like to follow an order if they have involvement in the creation of it. None of us likes to get orders only, rather everybody likes to be on driving seat and give the command.

Give People a Fine Reputation to Live Up To

It is a highly effective model to make people change others' behavior and attitude. If you want them to work on certain traits and polish them to be in a better state, just pretend to be the owner of the trait. Other people will be inspired and would strive hard to inculcate those traits.

If you want to improve a certain trait in other people, make it appear as though they already have that trait.

William Shakespeare quotes once that: "Assume a virtue if you have it not."

It holds good for other people. When we presume that the other person possesses a good feature which we feel they do not have presently, they will try hard to imbibe the reputation that you assume them to live up.

Chapter 10: What is the Importance of Analyzing People?

In the previous chapters, we have talked about how to analyze people and the importance of self-development to further assist in analyzing others. Since you have got a lot of insights into reading other people's personality; let us tell you why you need to analyze people and what is the significance of it.

Importance of analyzing

Analyzing means to examine or study something carefully in a methodical manner. If you analyze your children's report card, you may agree on their potency and weak point. In simple language, Analyzing people is reading a person's current state of mind, body, and emotions through your eyes. Analyzing varies from individual to individual as every individual has different perception or outlook to observe a trait in an individual but the conclusion would more or less similar if conducted on an individual. There is no formula to analyze people around or with you. Some people understand on the basis of their gestures, body language, verbal communication, nonverbal communication or the way he walks and dresses up.It comprises of primarily-

Studying yourself

 Understanding the nature of the person you are trying to analyze

 scrutinizing his behavior

Focusing on the words of another person

 Knowing body language

 Getting acquainted with cultural difference

 Concentrating on social skills

Forming a general assumption on the nature of a person

Interpretation of verbal communication and pattern

 Knowing the reason behind his type of personality

Having an elementary overview of the personality of an individual

Analyzing someone's personality requires deeper knowledge about many other things other than the ones mentioned.

Importance of understanding people

Why is it important to understand a personality? If you are ambitious, then yes it is important to read the other person but if you do not want any growth   professionally and happy with 9 am to 5 pm job then it is not your cup of tea. Likewise, if you value your relationships, analyzing folks is important. Analyzing people is of immense importance from the perspective of life more than any other realm like professionally.

More finely you understand yourself and other folks around, the more booming you will be in dealing with the circumstances and people and getting things on the right track. Understanding personalities is an unexpectedly comprehensive and practical subject than psychology. It is an extensive word comprising of psychology and implementing the analysis to day to day advantage in everyday circumstances. It is vital to stay with family and amongst friends as well as colleagues. Learn it, to be the best and different of all members of a group. Get it to attract people, to help, to support, to influence, to raise your voice and to express your point of view, to understand better, to make right and fast decision, to encourage people, to manage people, to direct folks, to solve the conflicts and most importantly to portray the right personality of ourselves.

Advantages of analyzing people

People are an open book needing little attention to understand their traits. On closely observing what they do, what they say and how they listen to others saying reveals a pretty good picture of their attitude and personality. It has proven to be effective and true in most of the cases. It is best that you can do as a friend, family member, colleague or a boss in the office. Analysis of people, their behavior, body language, and gesture is a fascinating phenomenon because of diverse learning experience based on traits or behavior adopted by a person. It is therefore significant and essential to be successful in distinct walks of life like a business arena, day to day life, companionships, relationships, etc.

Let us have a quick look at the advantage that results due to the analysis of people:

Analysis of people offers an individual the knowledge of skills required to deal with people. It mostly throws light on tips to conduct with positivity.

It assists to recognize, realize and uphold human life and its standpoint, thereby shun conflicts.

It helps an individual develop understanding and sympathy towards others and results in a reduction of   people from getting judgmental and restricts the person from pointing the finger at others.

It fabricates a healthy society enabling people to evaluate themselves before judging others.

Every individual to succeed in life requires important interpersonal and communication skills to be able to stand at a pioneering position in the corporate sector as well as in society which is always changing. In today's time when students and people are migrating out for jobs and studies, the study of the analysis of people is quite handy to understand people abroad and to minimize the possibility of deception.

Study of people is a type of preparation tool to cope up with the colleagues at the office and work efficiently at work front as well as social life.

It aids in comprehending the presence of imperfection in their life which can be improved by understanding the behavior of the other person and following his good features.

 We live in a society where people of different personalities, beliefs, attitudes, perceptions, and behaviors are found. Their analysis helps to get aware of the techniques to deal with them.

 It can be immensely helpful for   people at management level in picking up the right employees by understanding the behavior of their employees.

 Through analysis, you can project, direct, alter and control the distinct behavior of an individual

 Through analysis of people, you can get an idea of his reaction in a particular situation in advance and get prepared for the situation.

Analysis of people is helpful for the successful conduct of society and accomplishment of goals.

Chapter 11: How to Avoid Mistakes?

Mistakes. You think about them, talk about them, and lastly obsess regards to them. These mistakes help a human being to grow but, side by side they are very much embarrassing, shameful, and put companies to a great loss.

Everyone has the same old habit which they want to change by doing some mistake or the other. Actually, it is a part of human psychology to repeat the same behavior again and again. Therefore, changing the old behavior can be difficult but not impossible. It can only be eradicated by proper planning and staying positive while doing any work.

In human life, mistakes are very common things by which he/she learns a lot.

Sometimes when we work too much, some careless and silly mistakes will happen especially when you are doing your best. There isa number of examples of mistakes like sending an e-mail to the wrong person, overlooking a balance sheet, not ready for a presentation, and innumerable others.

Indeed, the person who is good at analyzing people easily judges whether the person has done some mistake or not by non-verbal communication channels.

Here you will come to know "How to avoid mistakes at work"?

First of all, acknowledge a mistake
Until and unless you fully appreciate what exactly has happened, till then it is impossible to avoid it. Some of the individuals are very hard at failure but forgot to re-examine what is to be done to avoid the mistake next time. So, keep these things in mind before doing any work: -
Don't be overconfident while doing any work as it leads to missing any information and you will tend to make a mistake
There are many bad habits which can be the reason of mistake so avoid any bad habit
Doing mistake means you are trying your best but do overdo it

Concentrate on what you are doing
Just focus on your own tasks and projects firsts. At the office, make work your priority and avoid any kind of activity while

doing office work. On the other hand, don't be a multitasked as it kills the overall productivity.

Moreover, start the work from the smallest and easy task and then take up a tough one.

Furthermore, at the start of the day give importance to those tasks which are significant.

Don't fear mistakes

This is one of the essential points in order to keep away from doing mistakes. Actually, the reality is in the fear of making a mistake, you try to be perfect but forget that by mistakes only you learn a lot.

In a study, it is considered that the human brain before doing any work sends a warning signal to prevent us from repeating the same mistakes again and again.

However, making mistakes is a good thing which eventually gives an opportunity to analyze themselves and others; but, up to some limit. So, do your work keeping past mistakes in mind.

Avoid distraction

Don't get distracted while doing any of the work in the office as it is prone to mistakes. Actually, distraction can take away your attention and make you jump between the task and the project. On the other hand, it also lowers down the overall productivity from your behalf.

Moreover, they create confusion and your attention will get split between two works. One essential step while doing office work is just put your phone aside as it is one of the most distracting things because of which end number of mistakes can happen.

Take the breaks at the appropriate time

If you work continuously then, it will harm your brain and it will not function in the right way. According to Harvard Business Review, if the person does overwork then the aging process will move faster, which as a result impact on memory and thinking skills.

So, to avoid this take some precautions like: -

Take some break while doing work and relax for some time

Talk to friends and relatives as it makes your brain relaxed and offer you a positive attitude of doing work

When you take a break in work, do something refreshing as it will activate your brain

Ask doubts and questions

The main reason formaking a mistake is having doubts about the assigned work because of their ego or are too afraid of asking. Most of the individuals think that what other people will think if they ask any doubt; but, they forget that if they do some mistake what another person will say about you. Now you can well assume that which one is essential for you.

Therefore, try to ask whatever comes in your mind with regards to the work. This, in turn, will be helpful in learning more about the task and can be very useful in completing your work on time without any mistakes.

Try to make a checklist

Checklists will help you to keep in track all the steps which you will do while completing a task. By following this process, your work will be full-fledged without any errors because you have taken care of every step by rechecking them again and again.

This checklist is also crucial for those individuals who are multitaskers and want to do multiple works at the same time. For them, it is very essential. And one of the crucial things in multiple tasking is don't leave any work incomplete otherwise you will lose the grip on that work.

Do external proofreading on your behalf

As an individual, if you have given your best in doing work then also cross-check the work again and again so that there are no chances of mistakes.

Try to analyze your work by taking the help of your manager, supervisor, or any experienced colleague.

Notwithstanding, getting a second eye on the work is a good method of improvising your work. And also, they make you understand overlooked errors which you are not able to understand.

Be clear with regards to your role in the organization

Do you know- what is the role you have been given by your company?

It is very essential to know this otherwise you will mess up all the things in order to complete every task.

On the other hand, surety of work offered to you makes you comfortable and that work will be mistake-free.

However, if you have any doubt about your duties and responsibilities then ask your boss to define it, and after that things will work much easier. In this case, there are no chances of errors.

Learn from every mistake which you will do

In case any mistake is done by you, don't blame it on others rather take the responsibility of that mistake for what you have done.

As an employee of any organization, learn from every error done by you and from others. Always make a note of all the mistakes done by you and by your colleagues and do the best effort not to repeat it again. Moreover, when you show a positive attitude towards the mistakes, then it will become a stepping stone of your success.

Indeed, this process makes you analyze yourself and others which are best for making strong relationships.

Always find the root of the mistake

Every human being makes mistakes but once it is done, taking precautionary measures so that it will not repeat again is mandatory.

If you want that this mistake will not happen again, then try to find out the root cause of the mistake.

After that think deeply about that issue and what are the steps you can take to prevent it further in the future. This will also help you to analyze your capability to get successful in life while observing others.

Try to have a healthy conflict

Mistakes are done by a single human being; but, in some cases, it might be due to conflicts between colleagues because of clashes in ego and opinions.

Make sure that you build a healthy relationship with each other so that every solution can be sought with the help of colleagues. Make yourself friendly and make a good rapport within the organization.

We all are human and mistakes are our part of life. The person who learns from the mistakes and tries not to repeat it is the best human being. So, with your own mistakes, you can analyze other individuals also the way they react and act to the mistakes and judge their personality.

Chapter 12: How to Spot Attraction, Romantic Interest, Insecurity, and Various other Emotions?

The attraction is something unusual which will happen anytime and anywhere. The question is how to know that- is someone attracted to you?

This question is very common among youngsters as they want to know what type of relationship they have with someone. The process of attraction also helps in analyzing a person in a better way. Let's talk about some of the clues by which you come to know that someone is attracted to you: -

Flirting as a sign of attraction

Sometimes, the person who is attracted by you send a flirting signal and then you will see what happens. In this process, try to be a little friendlier and if the opposite person reciprocates the energy then there is an attraction.

Moreover, if one person is using different techniques of flirting to express their interest then he/she may be interested in each other. Indeed, have confidence while you are sending flirting signals even though you are feeling shy as the saying says "fake it until you make it."

Body language

If the opposite person is making a lot of eye contact with you and also leaning towards you, then it might be an attraction. Their body language often shows nervousness like fidgeting or mimicking. However, based on body language, you can easily judge the person whether he/she is attracted to you or not.

Talk more with that person

Finally, direct interaction with that person is the surest way to know that someone is attracted by you. In case you think that there is a mutual relationship, then take that person alone for the conversation. Lead the issue slowly and then confess your feelings.

Always understand the limits of attraction

There are cases when someone is attracted to you but it is not sure that he/she wants to make a relationship with you. Actually, the attraction is a primal sensation.

This situation you cannot necessarily control what and how you feel it.

Test the waters

If you think that an individual is getting attracted to you, then try to find it more. In this case, be bold and little flirtatious and you might be able to bring more clarity to the situation.

Romantic Interest

Although, it is very difficult to spot romantic interest in you if you find that it is very easy for you to make the next move. Whether the man or woman is a long-time friend, paying attention to tell the signs of romantic interest which can easily reveal hidden feelings.

Just observe that person and try to analyze how he/she feels regards to you. The various steps of this process are: -
Observe the eye contact which you receive by that person. If you will receive eye contact which is full of emotions then it might include romantic interest.
Examine the body language of the person specially, non-verbal communication which is an essential aspect of deciphering an attraction
Observe how he/she pays attention to you when you are discussing the personal life. In this case, when he/she heard that you have a date with another person it might upset them and they also want to know about their hobbies.
Always pay attention to his desires which are best to please you.

Insecurity

If you're meeting with someone you just met, and after some time you feel that you started feeling insecure with that individual. Every human being suffers from insecurities like self-doubt, lack of confidence, and assurance which on the other hand influence human behavior.

To analyze people and your own insecurities will offer you a long-lasting benefit in any situation or relationships.

The below steps will surge your awareness regards to insecurities which as a result inspire your efforts to grow and deliver you step ahead in understanding others.

Someone who is insecure may shrink down a size if they are facing any social situation which cannot be controlled. They easily get themselves into stress, tension, fight, fall, and many more.

Eye contact is a form of non-verbal communication skill which enables people to understand and connect. But in case of insecure people, they sometimes have trouble making and maintaining eye contact.

According to the research it is stated that in another person's eye, you can easily read emotions such as happiness, sadness, and more than 50 mental states. So, it is also the best way to analyze people.

The person who is insecure always complains that things are not good enough.

When a person is putting him/herself into a position where they believe that they must defend him/her, in that case, they are showing insecurities by the way they react. Although when you watch closely, then you will come to know that person and his/her motive.

There are many examples of verbal communication by which anyone can analyze whether the person is feeling insecure or not.

The insecure person always feels that if they have done something wrong and start apologizing even though they have not done something

One of the serious signs of insecurity is they regularly feel like everyone dislikes them.

However, this is also another way of analyzing people by their verbal and non-verbal skills. So, being insecure is not an easy thing for a human being to live or to overcome. As an individual, being able to detect insecurity in the people around you can help you shake off self-doubts that some people seem to enjoy fostering in you.

Happiness

From all the other emotions, happiness is one of that emotion for which human beings strive a lot. It is that state which is featured by contentment, joy, gratification, satisfaction, and well-being. Indeed, this emotion will be expressed through facial expressions, body language, and tone of the voice.

However, these things are very essential to analyze whether a person is happy or not. The person who wants to master the art of analyzing people can easily judge the individual through these signs.

Sadness

Sadness is another type of emotion which is also called transient emotion. It has disappointments, grief, hopelessness, disinterest, and damped mood as their features. This emotion is experienced by everybody from time to time. A person who wants to read individuals can easily analyze by other person facial expressions whether he/she is sad or not.

Emotions and feelings play a very essential part of everyone's life, from influencing how effectively you engage with others in day to day chores. After understanding these emotions, attractions, and interest, we can take a deeper understanding of how it can be expressed and how to analyze a person with any of the emotion.

Chapter 13:" What is Psychology?

The term psychology is a very old term which is mainly used to study the human mind and behavior in order to analyze them. In this full analysis of human mind is studied, how it works, and most essentially how it affects the overall human behavior.

The American psychology association stated that psychology embraces all aspects of human experiences. This discipline is very multifaceted which is inclusive of many sub-fields in all sectors of life. But specifically, psychology is very helpful in reading people's mind. In the field of psychology, psychologists are persons who try to study people's mind.

But the truth is they don't read people, they have so much experience of meeting people under relatively closed conditions by which they may detect how human beings behave and think in different manners.

Here we will talk about some tricks related to mind-reading which numerous successful people have mastered. They are: -

Start with generational differences
First and foremost thing is that understanding the reading mind is understanding the generation in which they are living.

This one point will tell most of the thing regards to the human mind that how he/she thinks.

Moreover, it works as a lens between humans and their approach to see life. It tells us a lot about an individual's thinking, the motive of life, whether he/she thinks positive or negative, and innumerable others.

Try to recognize hot points of the individual

Secondly, the way to read a human mind is to look at the pain points of the person, which goes through asking questions concerning their personal and professional life. Because if you really want to make a strong personal bond, then what they consider regards to life is very essential.

The questions can be like-- what triggers emotions for them?

What are the things or situations that offer them comfort?

In this situation, psychologists make their ears big and mouth small. They usually start a conversation in a pre-planned manner so that the individual feels comfortable and relaxed.

Non-verbal decoding skills

In order to understand people and their feelings and emotions, non-verbal skills play a very essential role. So, watch the body language cues in the person. For example, if they are looking back, turning in and around, looking down, then they aren't interested in your talks. Other than this, if the person is answering you in a monotone; then also, they are most likely unattached to your concept. The psychologists easily understand these cues and come to the conclusion that what type of personality he/she has.

Be a good listener

Finally, listen to the person who is talking to you attentively which is the basic key to understand people's mind. Well, this concept will not work when you will talk to the person on the phone. So, reading people's mind is only possible when you directly listen to people with full concentration.

Now you come to know how beginners can start reading people's mind and make their relationships strong: -

Start opening up your spirits

In order to start reading people, open up your energy to the people and possibilities in and around you. Don't think anything else means the past experiences and or any conflicts which you want to read.

Keep in mind that you have to just present in front of that person keeping mind and soul at one point.

Seeing and not seeing

Whom you want to read, see that person and make a snapshot of his/her structure in your mind like the type of body, hair, eyes, and more. Make a mental column which will separate that person's traits and various other things that don't belong to that individual.

Focus on the person

Now what you have to do is just focus on the face of that person for around 15 seconds. Don't stare too long otherwise, it will make the person uncomfortable. After that, look away from that individual and feel what type of energy you possess from that person. You will become used to this technique with experience. Indeed, sit in silence and let feelings, emotions, and thoughts for that person fill your mind. Now let the actual process of mind-reading starts.

Begin with a conversation

At this point, you will uncover the personal thoughts and feelings which they think. Choose any topic for conversation which you like. Moreover, ask about their personal and professional life. Just keep in mind that the thoughts which are coming to your mind, the same will be in the mind of another person. This way you can immediately tell the person what he/she is thinking.

At last, I want to say that, the techniques of reading minds are what everyone can do, it's not about professional mentalists. In the starting, you might not get success in this field, but with practice, it can be easily attained.

So, best of luck on the path of reading people and give yourself a successful career.

Chapter 14: Individual Differences in People's Perceptions

We have already studied about the appearance, behaviors, and characteristics of the people we meet and usage of the above traits in understanding them. It is now vital to have an emphasis on social psychology on the situation of the people we decide to judge. A person is also vital, consequently, let us take into consideration a few of the person variables that affect our potency to judge the people.

Perceiver Characteristics

We believe that the outcome of an analysis of an individual conducted by different individuals will be the same as the concerned individual's behavior, nature and traits would be the same. For example, if you while discussing with your mom describe your sibling- say, Kitty, You both should have a similar opinion or almost similar description of her. But it may not turn out to be true in all cases, as the mom daughter relation is different from the relationship shared by the sibling. Kitty could be more demanding and stubborn to her mom than his elder brother/ sister.

In general, the equation of relationship, circumstances, frame of mind of an individual and the place of the meet are the few elements that will form the basis of analysis. The result will be different based on a distinct sample of behavior and would be surely different.

On the other hand, different impressions could be formed by individuals while talking to an individual. A human being usually uses his approach, schemas, experience, and expectations while forming an opinion about anyone. Interpretation of every individual will be different due to their own and distinct perception and this is what we like to substantiate on that our experience sketches the canvas of our perception.

One of the key elements that lay an impact over our opinion about a given individual is the way we observe the present cognitive accessibility of traits of a given individual. In other words, it can be said that the quickest image or idea that hits the perceiver about an individual too aids in forming different opinions about an individual. Due to variation inaccessibility, diverse people will get to see different aspects of one's personality. As some people emphasize on looks and dressing style of an individual, some would be captivated by physical stature, few by intelligence, etc. If your basic nature is inclined on your look, you too would first observe the dressing sense, branded stuff worn by him, etc.

This justifies our saying that the difference in accessibility leaves a mark over the type of impression that we form about others as we generate an idea on the things we focus on. However, if you ask a person to comment on some set of people, his observations would be more or less similar than on being asked by a different individual due to the difference inaccessibility of all people. If you are the one that stays attuned with the fashion, then the first criteria of observation would be on fashion sense or style only. Your opinion for others reflects a bit about your own persona too.

Need for cognition is the propensity to think comprehensively and vigilantly about our experiences. People can also be categorized in terms of their instinct to process information about others. Folks with a strong need for cognition engage in an intense and considerate manner and consequently may come out with more casual attribution and Vice Versa. People with a higher need for cognition emphasize more on circumstantial factors while taking into account the behavior of people. Such folks turn out to be more tolerant and lesser impulsive than those with lesser and no need for cognition.

Even though the need for cognition refers to an inclination to consider carefully and comprehensively about any topic, but there are also individual differences in the tendency of the people. Individual difference along with being present in our acknowledgment also hides in the kind of character that we construct about others and ourselves.

Few people can be sectioned into **entity theorists** who believed that traits are constant and not prone to change. Conversely, **incremental theorists** believe that traits and personalities vary with times. As per a study, people classified as incremental theorists more finely use the circumstantial aspects of the scenario than even actors. However, an entity theorist is also unable to encode the reasons for behavior. Individual differences in attribution styles also cast its impact on our own conduct. Entity theorists are presumed to face a tough time taking a new task as their own perception facilitates the thinking of inability to handle new challenges. An incremental theorist delivers better in new challenges as they consider themselves more flexible. You can notice how people's attribute can aid us to comprehend our perception about ourselves and others along with our attitude towards social context.

Attribution Styles and Mental Health

So far we have seen in this chapter that our ascription about other people has a great impact on our reaction. Along with making attributions about others, we also form attributions for our own behaviors. Social psychologists have revealed that in people, there are significant personage differences in the attribution that people craft to the pessimistic events that are experienced by them. These attributions can cast a huge influence on their reaction towards the other individual. This negative event can cause stress, anxiety, and depression on one individual, but at the same time may not have any effect on another person. Some may accept the challenge of a negative event and try the level hard to overcome the difficulty.

Attribution style indicates the type of attributions that we have a propensity to make for the events experienced by us. Attributions formed can be to due to our own internal or external characteristics. In addition to aforesaid causes, attributes can also be formed on facets involving stable vs. unstable and global vs. specific.

Stable attributions are those anticipated to be permanent, however unstable as the name suggests, are anticipated to change over time. Global attributions are the one that is applicable extensively, whereas specific attributions are those pertinent to a particular event only. The outcome of these negative attribution styles is desolation and bleakness. Studies reveal that school passes out students with negative attribution style first experienced depression than those with positive style during the initial months of college. Whereas, students with extreme negative attribution style are more prone to experiencing the learned helplessness.

Learned helplessness refers to the situation where due to the trouble experienced earlier, a person just surrenders even when he is out of the problem. For example- people exposed to excessive heat give up actually in protecting themselves when they can easily get under the shadow. Those who have undergone the experience of learned helplessness think that they do not have any control over the outcome and are where they get exposed to a range of health issues, along with depression and anxiety. Whilst there arepeople who tend to have a more positive attribution style. It is the mode of describing events concerned to high self-esteem and affinity to clarify the negative events experienced by them in context to external, unsteady, and explicit qualities.

Overall, it can be concluded that folks with positive attribution towards the negative events will confirm longer persistence in any task. These attributions can be valuable in better mental health to success in your field. However, it is not utterly fruitful. This strategy is associated with limitation too as it is literally impossible to have full control over everything and doing it can be nerve-racking. So, it is vital to develop an understanding of the state when you should give up and stop even thinking of it and just let things flow. This kind of positive and optimistic outlook is healthy; but at the same time, we should not develop unrealistic optimism in ourselves. Unrealistic optimism is the state in which we are nearly overconfident that we will overcome the negative things that we may come across. Too much of optimism may result in depression and failure when things do not go as per our anticipation. Over optimistic beliefs are risky.

The conclusion hereof connecting attribution style to mental wellbeing results to the interesting prediction that people's well-being can easily be improved by shifting from a negative to a (mildly) positive or optimistic attribution style.

These types of psychoanalysis have aided people in developing positive attribution style along with being quite effective in lessening obsessive-compulsive disorder, depression, and anxiety.

It has been highly useful in eradicating the Dysfunctional attributions amongst couples by encouraging them to develop positive communication and enhanced satisfaction from the relationship.

Attributions also play a significant role in establishing the quality of working relationships between clients and therapists in mental health settings.

The technique for the development of positive attribution style

Self-handicapping is a technique that is implemented and entails feeling people better about them. It occurs when we get involved in behaviors aiding us to build a suitable external attribution for likely failure. One of the two modes of self-handicapping ourselves is engaging in a form of pre-emptive self-attribution bias, whereas the second one involves behaving in a manner that makes success less possible. It can be a highly effective way of compromising with failure.

Benefits and harms are the two aspects of self-handicapping and let us unfold them one by one. If you fail after self-handicap, you can straightaway hold external affairs responsible for the failure and on succeeding. Despite handicap made by you only, you can hold your internal attributions reason for the success. On the other hand, getting involved in the behaviors that design self-handicapping can be pricey as it makes it tough for people to succeed. The result of research done on the people executes self-handicap frequently demonstrate a lower level of satisfaction in life, less aptitude, bad temper, uninterested in their jobs, and bigger substance mistreatment.

Luckily, the majority of folks maintain reasonable harmony between optimism and realism while drafting attribution for them and rely less on self-handicapping. Research reveals that fixing of reasonable goals and sentiments that we are moving towards gives us contentment, even if we may not accomplish the goals ourselves.

Key Takeaways

As our own expectations, people may build a distinct impression of an individual doing the same behavior.

Individual differences, on the other hand, in cognitive accessibility of a given personal trait may result in overlap in the description provided by a common perceiver regarding the same target individual.

Folks with a strong requirement for cognition make more casual attribution. The entity theorist pays more attention to the characteristics of the people, whereas incremental theorist has the propensity to believe that personalities change gradually.

Individual differences in attribution styles can leave their impact in the manner that we respond to the negative events experienced by us.

People with extremely negative attribution styles, in which they repeatedly make external, stable, and global attributions for their actions, are assumed to be experiencing learned helplessness.

Self-handicapping is an attribution technique that protects us from developing ability attributions for our own breakdown.

Having a positive outlook towards life and its event is healthy, but it should be tempered. We cannot turn unrealistic while listing the things we can and cannot do.

A quick Recap (Conclusion)

In the start of the book, we have discussed how to read people with the help of varied techniques and strategies which has become the demand of today's dynamic world. The situations around individuals demand a significant approach by which they can be successful in life. However, if an individual masters "How to Analyze People" then they can make quick decisions in life which can be beneficial.

As we have discussed throughout the book, human behavior is like the life script of an individual by which he/she can learn the art of reading people. Every human being whether the situation is bad or good tries to analyze people, and what they think regarding that issue. And up to some extent you may be right in reading people. Actually, it depends upon the type of human behavior we have.

The main purpose of this book is to help and aware readers to understand the importance of analyzing people through varied tricks like facial expression, body language, and numerous others.

However, we are grown-up individuals and have tremendous options to read people by learning and practicing different methods like by developing our personality, through social and communication skills, verbal communication, by analyzing different attractions, and many more.

Furthermore, there is so solo secret to analyze people, rather it comes only through learning and practicing. This concept makes your life more interesting and different which you will never think of. So, give your best in order to read people's mind and become an eminent personality.

In this book, all the concepts are explained related to how to read people, which ought to help the person to self-assess and understand the other people's behavior and why they react like this. Moreover, an individual would find this very beneficial to develop the art of observing and analyzing people so that over the period of time they easily understand people try to offer a suitable solution for their problems.